NELSON GUIDE TO

WRITING IN HISTORY

SECOND EDITION

JOY DIXON

University of British Columbia

JEFFREY W. ALEXANDER

University of Wisconsin—Parkside

NELSON EDUCATION

NELSON / EDUCATION

Nelson Guide to Writing in History, Second Edition
by Joy Dixon and Jeffrey W. Alexander

Associate Vice President, Editorial Director:
Evelyn Veitch

Editor-in-Chief, Higher Education:
Anne Williams

Executive Editor:
Laura Macleod

Executive Marketing Manager:
David Tonen

Developmental Editor:
Theresa Fitzgerald

Photo Researcher:
Jessie Coffey

Permissions Coordinator:
Jessie Coffey

Senior Content Production Manager:
Anne Nellis

Copy Editor:
Erin Moore

Proofreader:
Erin Moore

Indexer:
Belle Wong

Production Coordinator:
Ferial Suleman

Design Director:
Ken Phipps

Managing Designer:
Katherine Strain

Interior Design Modifications:
Olena Sullivan

Cover Design:
Olena Sullivan

Cover Image:
STOCK4B/Getty Images

Compositor:
Doris Chan

Printer:
Webcom

Library and Archives Canada Cataloguing in Publication

Dixon, Joy
  Nelson guide to writing in history / Joy Dixon, Jeffrey W. Alexander. —2nd ed.

Includes index.
1st ed published under title Thomson Nelson guide to writing in history by Jeffrey W. Alexander, Joy Dixon.

ISBN 978-0-17-650028-3

1. History—Research. 2. Academic writing. 3. Historiography.

I. Alexander, Jeffrey W. (Jeffrey William), 1972– II. Title. III. Title: Nelson guide to writing in history.

D13.D58 2009   907.2
C2008-907401-7

ISBN-13: 978-0-17-650028-3
ISBN-10: 0-17-650028-6

Contents

Contents

Preface to the Second Edition

This book began as a writing guide posted on the website of the History Department at the University of British Columbia. The original guide was produced in response to a demand from students, teaching assistants, and instructors in the department for a clear, easy-to-read, introductory guide to historical writing designed for Canadian students. It attracted attention from students and faculty not only across Canada, but also around the world. In 2006 we published an expanded and revised print edition of the writing guide, which gave us an opportunity to share this introduction with a larger audience. Since then, historical research and writing has been further transformed by the expansion of online and electronic materials and this Second Edition of the guide reflects those changes. Students and colleagues have also provided extensive feedback on what worked and what didn't work in the original guide, and we have made significant revisions to each chapter on the basis of those comments.

The *Nelson Guide to Writing in History* is aimed primarily at students taking their first university- or college-level history course. This is not a composition textbook or a grammar guide, and it is not a replacement for more comprehensive and technical style manuals. Our emphasis in this book is on what it means to think and write historically. We provide step-by-step instructions on how to cope with a variety of assignments that you are likely to encounter in your history courses, as well as an explanation of the technical elements of historical writing, such as how to use both primary and secondary evidence and how to properly document the claims you make in your historical writing. Most of all, we emphasize the importance of historical *argument*.

Throughout this guide, we have tried to use examples that are as similar as possible to real essay topics and real problems that you might encounter in your own course work. To give these examples more coherence and unity, we have developed four Sample Essays that reflect a range of approaches and historical specialties: one on the history of science and technology (the role of computers in the "space race"); one on European women's history (an analysis of Mary Wollstonecraft's *A Vindication of the Rights of Woman*); one on Native–newcomer relations in British Columbia; and one on the conflict between China and Japan between 1937 and 1945. The sample citations we provide are all drawn from actual works relevant to these topics.

Acknowledgments

The original, Web-based writing guide was the result of David Breen's initiative and energy as Head of the History Department at the University of British Columbia; without his commitment to developing resources to enhance student learning, this guide would not have existed. Joy Dixon was the chair of the committee that developed the original guide, and Jeff Alexander was the Web designer and author of that guide. We would like to thank all members of the History Department for comments and suggestions that assisted in the development of the original guide. One-third of the royalties from sales of this work go to support graduate education in history at the University of British Columbia.

Special thanks to Alejandra Bronfman, Paul Krause, Chris Friedrichs, and Bob McDonald for their advice and input, as well as to Maureen Ryan of the Department of Art History, Visual Art and Theory. We would also like to thank the staff at Nelson Education, especially Rod Banister, who saw this project through from its earliest stages to completion, and Amie Plourde for her development work on the project. For their work with us on the Second Edition, we are grateful to Roberta Spinosa and Theresa Fitzgerald. Thanks also go to the reviewers, whose comments and criticisms have enriched the work. Our sincerest thanks to Robin Anderson, University College of the Fraser Valley; Ernest LeVos, Grant MacEwan College; Tony Michael, University of Toronto; Andrew Thomson, Wilfrid Laurier University; Ken Cruikshank, McMaster University; George Hoffman, University of Regina; and Carolyn Podruchny. Finally, thanks go to our partners: to Hilary Mason from Joy Dixon and to Carolyne Albert from Jeff Alexander.

Introduction

I.I WHY WE WROTE THIS GUIDE AND HOW TO USE IT

University and college students have a wide variety of backgrounds and specialties, but many of you will study history at some point in your academic career. Whatever your major or specialization, we have written this guide with you in mind. Like other university and college instructors, historians appreciate research essays that are organized, argued, and written effectively. Historians also research, think, and write about the past in highly specialized ways, and we hope to give you as clear and concise an understanding of those specialized ways of thinking and writing as possible. If you pay careful attention to the instructions in this guide, and work to follow its recommendations in your own writing, we are confident that your writing can meet, and even exceed, your readers' expectations.

This guide provides a straightforward set of guidelines to help you to write a history research paper that is clear, coherent, and persuasive. It is a step-by-step account that will guide you in researching, organizing, and writing your essay. We have aimed to keep each section brief and to the point. There are many longer and more thorough style guides available, so if you have specialized or technical questions that are not answered here, you can consult some of the resources listed at the end of this guide, under "For Further Reading." If you want to learn how to write a history term paper or research essay without having to read a style manual that runs to hundreds of pages, then this guide is for you. In the next 90 pages or so, you will find a short introduction to the process of writing in history, as outlined below.

- We start with a discussion of what it means to write historically. A good history essay is not an opinion piece or a simple description of past events; it is an argument *about* the past written with careful attention to the historical evidence. A clear and forceful argument, well supported by appropriate evidence, is the single most important element in a successful history essay.
- In Chapter 1, we explore the many types of historical sources that are available to you, how they are classified, and how you should approach them.

- In Chapter 2, we discuss the various types of writing assignments common in history, along with their basic elements.

- In Chapter 3, we focus on the research essay and cover its component parts in detail. Using four Sample Essays, we provide illustrations of effective and ineffective organizational approaches, writing styles, and uses of evidence. Look for the "one thumb down," "one thumb up," and "two thumbs up" icons to find these examples. We have taken this approach because, after their assignments are graded, students often ask, "Why was my argument not clear?" or "What should have been included in my conclusion?" Rather than provide these answers after the fact, this guide aims to help you understand what is expected from a good essay before you begin—and how to approach each component of it in turn. This chapter also suggests practical ways to strengthen and clarify your argument and to ensure that you keep that argument clearly in view throughout the essay.

- Finally, in Chapter 4, we discuss citation format. Providing correct citations can be a boring and time-consuming process, but it is absolutely critical to the writing process in history. It allows your reader to appreciate the quality of your research and your careful acknowledgment of your sources. In this chapter, we also provide a series of sample citations for the most common kinds of historical sources, including electronic sources. The style manual we have used is *The Chicago Manual of Style* for the humanities (often referred to as "Chicago style"), the most commonly used style in historical writing.

Professional historians continue to work on their writing style throughout their careers—and behind every good author is a host of editors and colleagues who offer advice, corrections, and suggestions. Even good writing can be improved. Remember that the grade you receive on your history paper and the corrections and editing suggestions provided by your instructor are intended to help you improve your writing style and argue and document your case more effectively. Be receptive to these comments and discuss them further with your instructor if you need clarification. The best way to improve your writing is to keep practising and to keep getting feedback from your readers.

I.II WHAT IT MEANS TO WRITE HISTORICALLY

If you want to write effective and successful history essays, the most important thing you can do is learn to write like a historian. To do that, you need to understand and recognize the features that characterize history as a discipline. Just as a university or a college is organized into various departments, the different branches of learning are divided into disciplines. Each discipline has its own standards and conventions—there are different ways of thinking and writing that identify a piece of work as "history" or "literary criticism" or "sociology." While history shares many of the features of other disciplines in the humanities and social sciences, this guide is designed primarily to help you think and write historically and recognize the difference between historical and other kinds of thinking and writing.

Over the past few decades, many historians have begun to challenge traditional modes of historical thinking and writing, and the most recent histories are often heavily influenced by the insights of other disciplines. As you learn more about the discipline, you may come to share the concerns that these critics have developed. In order to develop an effective criticism of historical thinking and writing, however, you must first understand those elements that make historical work a valuable and distinctive contribution to learning.

Fundamental to the historian's approach is a concern with *change over time*. For some historians, emphasizing change over time means tracing the emergence of institutions, political systems, or ways of thinking over decades or even centuries. For others, it means emphasizing the radically different ways that members of previous societies understood the world, their place in it, and their relationships with others. Some of the most productive historical questions can emerge out of those moments when we encounter something in the past that seems strange to us or simply wrong by the standards of our culture; these are the opportunities for historians to begin to explore why and how the world has changed, so that something that once seemed so natural and convincing to people now seems artificial or inconsistent to us.

When historians examine a text, an artifact, or an image from the past, our primary concern is to decide what it can tell us about the place and the time that produced it. So, for example, if we are studying late-eighteenth-century writings on women's rights (an example we will be returning to later in this guide), the point is not to argue *with* our sources over whether or not they were "right" in their views on women's roles and responsibilities, but to create an argument *about* those views.

As historians, we strive to understand and explain the actions, behaviours, and beliefs of women and men in past societies. This is not to say that we should never take a stand on the events and ideas of the past. Many historians have strong intellectual, ethical, or political views that help shape the questions that inform their work. At the same time, good historians are aware that while contemporary concerns may help us develop new questions about the past, they cannot provide us with historical answers.

The most significant and productive historical debates are often over the kinds of questions we can or should ask of the material. The history we write is not just an account of "what happened" in the past. It is also a claim about what is *important* about what happened and about how we should go about doing history. Different fields of history—social history, economic history, intellectual history, and military history, to give only a few examples—represent different approaches to the past. They use different explanatory models and make different assessments about appropriate use of evidence. Is a history of home and family life as important as a history of political institutions? Is the story of colonialism enriched by including the voices of First Nations peoples? Should historians make an effort to use nontextual sources in their work? If so, what techniques should they use to accomplish these things? There are no universally accepted answers to these questions. You may find that one instructor's advice or approach directly contradicts what you are taught in another course. Learning to recognize and understand different assumptions about the practice of history is an invaluable skill. While historians sometimes disagree about "what happened," those disagreements are often, if not always, linked to these larger questions. Asking these kinds of questions is an important part of what it means to think and write historically.

Historical Sources

Astronaut Buzz Aldrin walks on the moon
during the Apollo 11 mission, 20 July 1969.
The photo was taken by fellow astronaut
Neil Armstrong.
NASA

INTRODUCTION

Historical research is a kind of detective work, and knowing where to search for clues and how to weigh their importance is often like piecing together a puzzle—or a crime scene. Many major historical persons, ideas, and events are well documented, but many more are not. Historians are faced with partial, fragmentary, and often contradictory evidence and they use it to build up a more or less convincing picture of the past. They can then write about and discuss their interpretation of history based upon those clues, thus contributing to our understanding of the past. Not every puzzle is easy to solve, but getting started requires some understanding of the wide variety of historical sources available to you.

Before we explore these sources and discuss how they should be approached we should first be clear both about the nature of historical research and about the process of reading your source material. When you are researching the past, the methods and the sources that you choose can vary widely, depending on the topic that you are investigating. Some historians work with very old documents found in archives and libraries, while others conduct interviews or examine visual sources in order to investigate the past. Your particular research project may not rely on these techniques, or research methodologies, but it is important to keep in mind that there are a variety of possible approaches. All historians, however, are limited by the nature of the available sources. There are many important areas where source material is inadequate or even nonexistent. In this chapter, we outline the principal types of historical sources that are most likely to be available to you. We also discuss how these sources are classified, how they differ, and how they should be used.

When it comes to sources, students sometimes find that the amount of reading in history courses is overwhelming, but you should keep in mind that *how* you read is just as important as *what* you read. If you include a dozen books and articles in the bibliography of your research essay, your instructor will not expect you to have read every single page closely and carefully. The sources you have chosen could total thousands of pages, many of them irrelevant to your topic.

Rather than getting bogged down in the details of the evidence presented in a book or article, you should first try and read *conceptually*. Look for the "big picture," or conceptual framework, and pay attention to *how* the authors use evidence, as well as to the evidence itself. Sometimes, it helps to read the material twice—once to scan for the big picture and a second time to focus on the evidence relevant to the paper that *you* want to write. Take the time to read and think about the material carefully. Critical reading like this simply cannot be done at the last minute, just before your paper is due. You will need time to consider the argument you want to make in your essay. Ideas for research often come at the oddest times, and if you have enough time before the deadline to digest the material you have read, you are more likely to be able to develop an interesting and sophisticated argument.

Historical sources come in a wide variety of styles and formats and are generally divided by historians into two types. *Primary sources* are the earliest sources on a topic, and they provide the most immediate, first-hand accounts of the events or movements historians study. *Secondary sources* are later accounts based upon primary sources. They are written after the fact to interpret the events of the past for a new generation. There are, however, no hard-and-fast distinctions between primary and secondary sources. For example, if you were studying the French Revolution, then Thomas Carlyle's *The French Revolution: A History*, first published in London in 1837, would be a secondary source (though not one we would recommend, given its age). If you were studying English attitudes to revolution in the 1830s (a time of considerable political unrest) then Carlyle's study would be a useful primary source.

In the next two sections (1.1 and 1.2) we discuss these two kinds of sources in more detail. In the second part of this chapter we explore new ways of accessing material (especially online), different kinds of primary sources (visual sources, oral histories, artifacts and material culture, for example), and different ways of presenting and organizing information (for example, in tables or maps).

1.1 PRIMARY SOURCES

Primary sources are those that were produced or recorded in the era that you are researching. They may include diaries or personal journals, letters or telegrams, books or autobiographies written by contemporary figures (people who lived in that era), court transcripts or police records, newspaper or magazine articles, or government documents, such as law codes or transcripts of parliamentary proceedings. Recorded speeches and interviews or their transcripts (a written version of what was recorded) are also important primary sources. Other less conventional primary sources include laboratory notes, ships' logs, inscriptions, and photographs. Some historians also work with folk tales, oral histories or legends, works of art, or song lyrics. Virtually anything produced at the time you are studying can become a primary source in your historical investigation. Most university libraries have a wide variety of primary source material. Some of that material may be in a "rare books" or "special collections" division of the library and you may need special permission to access it. Because this material is often fragile there may also be restrictions on how much can be photocopied or how it can be handled. Many libraries also have extensive collections, including copies of newspapers and magazines dating back to the eighteenth century, available on microfilm and microfiche. If you find a valuable article, many microfilm readers can print copies for you for a small fee, or even create a digital document. Be sure to note all of the publication information, such as date, issue, and volume. (Remember that one reel may contain many different sources or issues of a periodical, so be careful to cite the correct source.) More and more libraries are also acquiring collections like Early English Books Online (EEBO), which includes digital facsimiles of over 125,000 printed books dating back to the 1400s. (See section 1.3 for more discussion of online sources.) Talk to your instructor or to a subject librarian about the digital collections that would be most useful for the papers you are writing.

Primary sources are the "raw materials" that historians use to create a new understanding of the past. They enable us to discover what people were doing, planning, or discussing at a particular time and place. When such sources are put into a larger context, such as a historical investigation into a particular event or social trend, they can provide valuable information. At the same time, it is important to remember that these sources are not transparent windows into the past. The primary sources we have access to are already the product of a long historical process in which some materials were preserved and others were not. This is why we have much more material to tell us about the lives and concerns of the wealthy and powerful, for example, than we do for the less powerful. We should also remember that each primary source provides only a partial record of the past. So, while a private diary might reveal a hidden opinion or unknown event, we should keep in mind that it was still written for an audience, though it may have been an audience of just one. Even diarists organize their material in certain ways, and this shapes their stories and their narratives. Autobiographies can also provide invaluable insight into events, but they might attempt to alter the historical record in their authors' interests.

You must also be careful when approaching sources written by people who were close to the events they described. It is not just that memories may be unreliable; authors may also have emphasized or de-emphasized particular details. If you were writing an autobiography of your own life, would you tell readers about all of your most embarrassing moments or describe your faults in detail? The tendency for major figures from the past, such as revolutionary leaders or politicians, to gloss over their less successful ventures when writing about their own lives may have been even greater. Similarly, they might have chosen to portray their contemporary rivals negatively, or perhaps leave them out altogether. Be aware of an author's possible interests in discussing or avoiding certain subjects.

Government documents can provide important information such as the text of legislation, social statistics, or transcripts of parliamentary debates. Like other kinds of primary documents, however, they should not be viewed as a direct reflection of the past. Examine such documents critically, considering the nature of the era in which they were produced and the audience for whom they were written.

Similarly, newspaper reports and articles are often influenced by the political atmosphere of the time. The information and analyses that they provide must be weighed carefully alongside other sources. Journalists do not have the benefit of hindsight to help them draw their conclusions about the present. Thirty years after a story appeared in the newspaper, new information has probably come to light, and the article's contemporary assumptions may appear incorrect—or even ridiculous. It is important to remember that earlier authors may not have had access to as many sources—or as many sides of the story—as we have today.

Another type of primary source is the novel, which is often dismissed by many students because they believe that "it's fiction—it's not about anything that really happened." Novels, like political works, can also engage in contemporary debates, and some instructors may focus writing assignments on such sources. Novels can tell us about their authors' concerns and assumptions, as well as the kinds of issues that preoccupied writers in various eras. Of course, we have to remember that the author has made specific decisions about how to portray the characters. Therefore, we must be careful not to confuse what the novel's narrator or characters say with what the author was actually thinking. The author may have chosen to create characters with radically different opinions than those he or she held. If your instructor has not specifically instructed you to use or to write about novels in your assignment, ask before including them in your research. Fictional works can be useful historical sources, but interpreting them can be challenging.

1.2 SECONDARY SOURCES

Secondary sources are based on or derived from primary sources, and they are typically produced by scholars investigating particular historical topics. Many different kinds of secondary sources exist. History textbooks offer broad surveys and most are not based on original historical research. Instead, they summarize the work of many historians to produce a synthesis that reflects the current state of the field. Encyclopedias and historical dictionaries (sometimes described as "tertiary" or third-order sources) are even farther removed from original research and scholarship, and are usually summaries of secondary sources aimed at a general audience. They can give you a useful overview of a topic or a convenient way to check names and dates, but they do not provide the kind of information and argument that you will need for university- or college-level work. Historical monographs (books written about one thing) are more narrowly focused, and newer monographs often challenge or revise the conclusions found in textbooks. Other secondary sources include anthologies or collections of articles, written by a number of authors about a subject or subjects, and articles in academic journals. Documentary films and museum exhibits provide another source for information about the past, although they are usually aimed at broader or more general audiences than other academic work. After sifting through a lot of primary evidence—like autobiographies, speeches, or government records—the authors of secondary sources are able to draw a series of broader conclusions about the past. For example, the individuals involved in a large event, like a world war, were typically participants in only a small part of the action, but the author of a secondary source can combine the writings or recollections of several dozen participants to form a larger picture of the nature of the conflict. Through such a composite analysis, conclusions may be drawn about the impact of the war on anything from world oil prices to the role of women in wartime production, depending on the sources consulted and the author's interests.

Finally, remember that secondary sources do not always agree. They are contributions to an ongoing debate, and they may be written from very different perspectives. Secondary sources aim to revise, challenge, or amplify existing ideas about the field, so you need to be aware of the position that each author has taken in relationship to other works in the area. Always read your sources with care and be sure to identify correctly who is making the claims you cite. Your choice of secondary source material will have an impact on the nature of your investigation and of your argument. Consult your instructor if you have any questions about your sources.

Here is a checklist to help you identify and read your secondary sources:

- *Check who wrote the work.* Are they professional historians? Information about the university with which they are affiliated or the training they have received can help you answer this question. If the book or article was published by a university press or a trade press that is well known for its academic publications, it has probably gone through the process of peer review, in which experts in the field are asked to evaluate and comment on the work before it is published. More general, "popular" histories can often provide useful overviews, but they may not deal with the kinds of questions that interest professional historians.

- *Check when the source was first published and whether it has been revised since.* If the source is more than 15 years old, it is likely that newer sources on the same topic have been published. Older works often remain very useful, but keep in mind that further research may have yielded newer details and interpretations. Keep an eye out for more recent works on the same subject. These often appear in academic journals.

- Read the introduction. It often summarizes the contents of the work and provides an outline of the author's arguments. The editors of collections of articles often provide a summary of each chapter in the work; reading these summaries can be a very good way to determine if the source is useful to your research.

- *Check the table of contents* and identify which parts of the source are worth reading in detail. Read through those parts and take notes. You may be surprised by how useful some of your early findings end up being to your research. As always, keep track of where you found a certain fact or passage.

- *Check the index* for further entries concerning certain persons, events, or concepts that you are researching. Sometimes, the author may discuss certain figures in several different places throughout the work, and the index will help you find those entries.

- *Read the conclusion.* In it, the author, authors, or editors will have summarized the arguments and the findings within the work and will often have made suggestions for future research. Some of these questions may give you additional ideas for your own paper.

- *Look at the bibliography.* This is where authors list all of the sources they have examined when researching and writing their own work. Some of these might be very obscure or located in distant libraries but many of the secondary sources listed will probably be available in your own university's library. Decide which ones might be useful and track them down as well.

- *Take your time.* As you read your sources, you will discover things about them that are interesting or controversial, one of which could form the basis of your thesis. (See section 3.4 for details about writing a thesis statement.) Think about these issues and isolate what it is about the topic that you want to use to develop your argument. This process may take a few hours each day for several days. Talk about the subject with others if you can—sometimes their opinions or questions can be inspiring.

1.3 ONLINE SOURCES

In the past dozen years, a wide variety of electronic media sources have come into use by people in many professions, including historians. Valuable sources of information, such as government documents, statistics, and bibliographic references, are now available in electronic format. Many sources formerly available only in print have recently been digitized and made available to users on the Internet. Online libraries, like Questia (at **www.questia.com**), provide electronic versions of many print texts, and databases like Project Muse® (at **muse.jhu.edu**) offer online versions of many print journals.

The library website at your institution probably provides access to a wide variety of online academic journals, known as electronic journals (or e-journals), and many historical journals are among them. Authors of articles featured in such sources are typically professional historians, and their work is usually peer reviewed, which means that an editorial committee and a series of experts in that particular field have examined it for credibility and accuracy. An index of e-journals can be found on most university or college library websites, and one of the best ways to search for articles relevant to your topic is by searching a database like JSTOR or Academic Search Premier. Many people are unaware that search engines like Google search only about one-third of the Web, but search engines like Academic Search Premier are able to search the "deep Web," where the real, full-length scholarly articles are. University and college libraries pay subscription fees to access these databases, which enable you to download, save, and even print the full text of articles written by historians and published in a wide variety of journals and other media. This is the sort of online research your instructor wants you to perform, and since your tuition dollars help to make these resources available, you should take advantage of them. Your library's staff will be glad to help you search for articles on your topic using these powerful tools.

There are also many useful databases managed by local or national governments. In Canada, the federal department of Library and Archives Canada hosts an excellent website entitled ArchiviaNet, which contains links to dozens of textual and visual sources such as diaries, memoirs, census data, and colonial archives. Visit **www.collectionscanada.ca** and follow the links to ArchiviaNet to view the collection.

There are also some commercial search engines focused on scholarly material that can be helpful at some stages of your research. Google Inc. has launched a search engine called Google Scholar (at **scholar.google.com**), which allows you to search for documents, papers, and publications produced by scholarly, governmental, and institutional researchers, among others. Google Scholar is a "meta-search engine," which means that it combines results from many of the sources we have listed above. It screens out most non-academic material and can be a useful way to find book reviews or articles quickly. Like other search engines, though, the information it provides is only as good as the keywords that you enter, so you need to use it carefully in order to find relevant material. Google has also recently announced plans to scan the public-domain print materials of the Michigan, Stanford, Harvard, and

Oxford University libraries and make them available online under the name Google Print. For further information, visit **print.google.com/ googleprint/library.html.** Initiatives like this make it possible for students and scholars to access rare material at some of the world's finest research libraries from any computer terminal, opening up exciting new possibilities for historical research.

While online sources can be very useful and access to them is increasing, the value and accuracy of these sources can vary widely. When consulting sources online, consider the nature of the publications you encounter. Are they Web-based academic journals or government databases, or are they popular websites hosted by private individuals? You can often tell the difference between an academic site and a popular site by its Web address. Those sites that end with ".edu" are hosted by universities in the United States, while those ending in ".com" are commercial sites. If you examine a popular website, pay attention to the credentials of the person or group hosting it. Also check the publication date of the site and the date of the last update.

Many websites about historical events or subjects are available, but be careful when examining their contents. If they make bold or innovative claims without providing reference to source materials or evidence, their arguments may be unsubstantiated and unreliable. Be suspicious of radical, revisionist interpretations of historical events or of conspiracy theories that cannot be supported by reliable evidence. Well-researched and well-written histories will always provide the reader with references to the sources used.

You should also avoid conducting serious research based upon what you find at online sources like Wikipedia. Like any encyclopedia, Wikipedia can be a useful starting point when searching for research topics, and it can be helpful for looking up simple information like key historical dates, but you should never base your paper on Wikipedia entries. Because Wikipedia is a user-edited encyclopedia you also need to remember that the reliability of its entries can be very uneven. Many Wikipedia entries are well researched and documented, but the best entries are usually ones that reference published sources (in print or online) by experts in the field. Take the time to find those works and read them for yourself. Your library will have many of those sources, and it can order virtually any other source from other libraries. In any case, many instructors will not allow students to cite Wikipedia as a source, so you are better off tracking down published material that has been written, reviewed, and edited by professional historians.

Be careful to cite your use of legitimate online sources very carefully and to observe the proper conventions for quoting or paraphrasing such material. Examples of proper citation format for online sources appear in section 4.4, on page 89. *The failure to cite online sources correctly constitutes plagiarism,* which is a serious and punishable academic offence, so be certain to acknowledge all of the online material that you consulted when researching and writing your paper. See section 4.2 for further details on plagiarism and how to avoid it.

Other valuable online resources are the article databases kept by major periodicals such as the *New York Times* newspaper or *The Economist* magazine. The *Times,* for example, allows you to search for articles dating back to 1851, which makes it a valuable source for U.S. history. Occasionally, these periodicals require a small fee to access or to reproduce a particular article from a back issue, but if the article is unavailable in your local college or university library, paying this fee may be a useful option.

Below are further links to useful online sources on a variety of historical topics and areas.

African History

- An A–Z of African History on the Internet
www.lib.msu.edu/limb/a-z/az.html
This comprehensive index of online resources on African history is hosted by Michigan State University.
- Africa, South of the Sahara
www-sul.stanford.edu/depts/ssrg/africa/history.html
This site, hosted by Stanford University, offers an extensive list of links to Internet resources on African history.

Ancient and Medieval History

- Internet Ancient History Sourcebook
www.fordham.edu/halsall/ancient/asbook.html
This index provides links to a wide variety of online, print, and archival resources on the ancient and medieval history of Europe and the Near East.
- The Labyrinth: Resources for Medieval Studies
labyrinth.georgetown.edu
This site offers links to numerous databases, services, texts, and images of interest to researchers of medieval Europe.

Asian History

- Asian Studies WWW Virtual Library
coombs.anu.edu.au/WWWVL-AsianStudies.html

This page provides links to online, print, and archival resources of use to researchers investigating the history of Asia.

• East Asian Libraries Cooperative WWW
pears.lib.ohio-state.edu
This index includes links to online sources related to Asian, Chinese, Japanese, Korean, and Manchu studies.

Canadian History

• Library and Archives Canada
www.collectionscanada.ca
This resource provides access to thousands of documents, records, films, maps, and periodicals of interest to all researchers of Canadian history.

• AMICUS
www.collectionscanada.ca/amicus
This database allows you to search over 30 million published records from 1,300 Canadian libraries, including Library and Archives Canada.

• Early Canadiana Online
www.canadiana.org/eco
This digital library contains over 1,800,000 pages in more than 12,850 volumes. It features published works from the time of the earliest European settlements to the beginning of the twentieth century.

• WWW-VL History: Canadian History
vlib.iue.it/history/CANADA/canada.html
This index provides links to a wide variety of online, print, and archival resources on Canada's history.

• CBC Archives
archives.cbc.ca
This online archive features audio and audio-visual clips from CBC Radio (from the 1920s to the present) and CBC Television (from the 1930s to the present).

European History

• The WWW-VL European History Project
vlib.iue.it/history/europe.html
This website, hosted by the European University Institute (EUI), includes extensive resources on European national histories, as well as the history of Europe as a whole.

• The European Integration History Index
vlib.iue.it/hist-eur-integration

This site features online sources on European integration since the Second World War in various languages.

Latin American History

* LANIC
lanic.utexas.edu/la/region/history
The Latin American Network Information Center, hosted by the University of Texas, offers links to a wide variety of Web-based resources of use to researchers studying the history of Latin America. Many of them are in Spanish.
* WWW-VL History Central Catalogue
vlib.iue.it/history
Scroll down to "Americas" for links to historical sources concerning individual countries in Latin America.

U.S. History

* The Library of Congress: American Memory Collection
memory.loc.gov/ammem
This page is a gateway to the library's vast collections.
* The History Cooperative
www.historycooperative.org
This online collection of scholarly journal articles on a wide array of subjects has been created by the American Historical Association (AHA), the Organization of American Historians, the University of Illinois Press, and the National Academies Press.

1.4 VISUAL SOURCES

While many historians work primarily or even exclusively with written texts, those influenced by disciplines such as anthropology, art history, or cultural studies have begun to expand the range of primary sources they use in their work. Like the written texts we discussed above, nontextual sources, such as portraits, political cartoons, photographs, and films, do not simply reflect the world in which they were written. Like written texts, these visual and aural "texts" amount to interventions in contemporary debates—meaning that they worked to produce, challenge, or reinforce assumptions about the people and events portrayed in them. They can be an important source for historical research.

Visual sources can be found in a variety of places. A good starting point is your own institution's library catalogue. Many university libraries have a department of special collections that includes very old or rare photographs, prints, artwork, and portraits. These sources are often delicate, and they are available to be viewed with a librarian's assistance. Talk to your instructor and ask how visual sources relating to your topic can be incorporated into your paper.

There is also a wide variety of visual source material that has been scanned and made available online. Be careful when using Internet source material; begin your search through your library's online catalogue or through a government or university website. An excellent place to start is ArchiviaNet, hosted by Library and Archives Canada at **www.collectionscanada.ca** (follow links to ArchiviaNet). This resource provides access to archival holdings from both private and governmental sources, including maps, photographs, videos and films, architectural drawings, sound recordings, and stamps and medals.

When you look at an image, you should ask many of the same questions you would ask of written primary sources. Who created it and when? Where did it first appear? Who was the intended audience? Keep in mind, however, that the analysis of visual imagery also requires you to ask different kinds of questions, such as, What elements of the image are foregrounded? and How does the artist use light and shadow to highlight or obscure various parts of the image? Be particularly attentive to the juxtapositions of image and text in a source; elements that are obscured or marginalized in the text may figure more prominently in the image, and vice versa. Sometimes, the image comments on or even undermines the message of the text itself.

FOR EXAMPLE: Here is a plate from Captain James Cook's *A Voyage to the Pacific Ocean*, published in London in 1784. This image, "A View of the Habitations in Nootka Sound," was an engraving of a work by the artist John Webber, who accompanied Cook on his third voyage.

We know that this image was created in the context of a voyage that combined scientific exploration with European colonial expansion. How does this image work to tell a particular version of the encounter between Native peoples and Europeans? The artist has chosen to portray a peaceful scene in which the newcomers appear to be welcomed by an admiring crowd. The artist has also used a variety of techniques to make the two English officers prominent in the image. Their light coats make these officers (one in the small boat on the lower right of the image and one just to the left of the centre of the image) stand out against the darker background, more visible than either the villagers or the ordinary English seamen. The strong diagonals created by the sailboat and canoe on the right side and the single canoe on the left intersect where the

John Webber, "A View of the Habitations in Nootka Sound," from James Cook, *A Voyage to the Pacific Ocean* (London: W. & A. Strahan, 1784).

Courtesy of Royal BC Museum, BC Archives (Image PDP00234)

English officer stands leaning on his rifle, symbol of English military power. Far from being a realistic and objective picture of an actual event, Webber's drawing makes a complex set of claims about European power and the "superiority" of European culture.[1]

Films can also make useful historical sources. Like novels, films engage in contemporary debates and tell us useful information about the kinds of issues that filmmakers were concerned with in a particular era. While novels usually have a single author, they are still collaborative efforts, involving publishers, editors, copy editors, and publicists, as well as readers. Filmmaking is even more obviously collaborative, involving not only producers and directors but also script writers, actors, sound engineers, lighting designers, publicity agents, and others who make important contributions to the finished product. When viewing a film as a historical source, you need to be attentive to many different issues, from casting decisions to the use of lighting and soundtrack.

You can also find a wide variety of fascinating and useful film clips online. News organizations like the BBC or CNN have Web-based archives that can be accessed without charge. The British Pathe Film Archive (**www.britishpathe.com**) carries material dating back to 1896. The Vanderbilt Television News Archive (**tvnews.vanderbilt.edu**) includes material from U.S. broadcasters from 1968 to the present, much of which can be accessed online by students from subscribing institutions or borrowed (for a fee) on DVD or VHS. You can also find material on user-generated content sites like YouTube (**www.youtube.com**), although copyright issues often make key material unavailable there. If you were writing a paper on the origins of the Cold War, for example, you could watch a series of contemporary newsreel films describing the Soviet Union's launch of the Sputnik satellite in 1957 and its impact in the West. Similarly, if you were writing a paper on the Cuban Missile Crisis, you could watch President John F. Kennedy's famous televised address to the American public that aired on 22 October 1962. Many events since the Second World War were documented in newsreels and television broadcasts, and you can quote or simply paraphrase them in your paper, provided you cite your sources as accurately as possible. If you are unsure, ask your instructor which kinds of contemporary films are worthwhile sources.

---

[1] Indigenous accounts of this encounter tell a quite different story. You can find a useful discussion of this issue in Daniel Clayton, "Captain Cook and the Spaces of Contact at Nootka Sound," in *Reading Beyond Words: Contexts for Native History*, 2nd ed., ed. Jennifer S. H. Brown and Elizabeth Vibert (Peterborough: Broadview Press, 2003), 133–62.

1.5 ARTIFACTS AND MATERIAL CULTURE

Anything made by human beings is an *artifact*. In this context, we want to use the term to draw attention to the material dimension of human productions. (In some historical writings, as well as in certain anthropological and archaeological ones, "artifacts" are opposed to "art," and the term "artifact" is used to denigrate the productions of Aboriginal peoples and other marginalized groups. This use of the word "artifact" should be avoided.) Things like buildings, tools, kitchen utensils, and industrial machinery are all examples of artifacts that can tell us important things about the societies that produced them.

Written and visual sources also have a material form that can provide important historical information. Looking at a book should involve paying attention to its physical properties—that is, its form as well as its content. We can ask the following questions: What kind of paper was it made out of? Were the materials used to produce it rare and costly, or was it made to be sold cheaply? What size was it? Was it a book to be curled up with in private or an imposing volume to be read in public? Was it richly illustrated or dense with text? The answers to these questions can tell us a lot about the intended audience as well as about the ways that the author or publisher intended the work to be read. A more expensive book would probably be aimed at an elite audience, and the work itself might be valued as much for the way it displayed the wealth of the owner as for its content. An inexpensively produced book with relatively simple text and many illustrations might be intended for a broader, less well-educated audience. Think about the ways in which the layout affects the connections that a reader can make or about the physical relationships between written text and visual imagery on the page.

We can also examine physical objects such as buildings or tools to see the kinds of historical relationships promoted by or characteristic of the society that produced them. In early modern Europe, for example, most houses were built without hallways and without clearly differentiated spaces for eating and sleeping. By the nineteenth century, wealthier families had begun to design and build houses that allowed them to separate different activities. There were special rooms dedicated to eating, cooking, socializing, and sleeping. Strict divisions were maintained between the servants' quarters and the rooms used by the family. Children and adults occupied different parts of the house, and in some cases separate areas were introduced for men (gun rooms, libraries, smoking rooms) and women (boudoirs, dressing rooms, drawing rooms). The architecture of these houses conveyed important messages about wealth and social status, both within the family and within society as a whole.[2] Similarly, we can find important clues to the power relationships within past societies in the layout of a factory floor or a sports stadium. Archaeological evidence can also be crucial, especially when we are studying cultures that have not left written records. Careful excavations of middens (places where day-to-day waste is collected, sometimes over generations) have provided critical information about topics as diverse as the agricultural practices of First Nations communities and the religious practices of slaves in plantation societies.[3] Similarly, landscapes themselves not only have a history, but they also reflect the historical activities of earlier generations. We can find evidence of transportation and communication networks, agricultural techniques, religious rituals, or attitudes to the natural world in the ways that human beings have reshaped the land. The important point is to think about these artifacts and spaces historically and to try to understand how they would have been used or inhabited.

1.6 ORAL HISTORIES

One of the reasons why historians have begun to look for sources other than written texts is that for most of human history written sources have reflected the perspective of the most educated and most powerful sections of society. Historically, women, the working class, and Aboriginal peoples have been underrepresented in written sources. In the 1960s and 1970s, many historians became interested in doing history from the "bottom up"; with the new interest in social history and women's history came an interest in oral histories, in which the life stories of ordinary men and women were recorded and (in many cases) transcribed. Some oral histories are first-person narratives, while others are produced through interviews conducted by researchers or other interested people. Many university archives contain sound recordings and transcripts of these stories and exchanges, and these can provide an invaluable perspective on historical events. Oral histories have become particularly important—and controversial—in First Nations history, and a sophisticated literature has developed over the place of oral histories in that field.

---

[2] For an exploration of these themes, see Leonore Davidoff and Catherine Hall, *Family Fortunes: Men and Women of the English Middle Class, 1788–1850* (Chicago: University of Chicago Press, 1987), 357–96.

[3] The excavation of burial sites and analysis of human remains can also provide important information to historians, but these kinds of excavations are increasingly criticized and opposed by those who see them as a desecration of sacred space.

Like written accounts, oral histories need to be used carefully. Because they are often generated years after the event, the stories they tell have often been shaped and reshaped over time. Memories of the Second World War, for example, may have been influenced by films or documentaries or by conversations with other participants. The perceived significance of past events can change as contemporary circumstances change. Oral histories also pose their own special problems of interpretation. As you read the transcripts or listen to the recordings, you should be aware of the role of the interviewer. What kind of relationship existed between the interviewer and interviewee? Did the interviewer use questions that made it difficult for the interviewee to respond freely? If you are working from transcripts, there are other questions to ask. Who transcribed the interview from its recorded audio format into text, and how much has the interview transcript been edited? What features of the interview—tone, body language, context—have been lost in the process of transcription? These are important questions.

You may also want to produce your own oral histories by conducting interviews. If you do, you will need to prepare carefully in order to know what questions to ask and to be able to recognize the significance of the stories you are told. You should also remember that your presence will affect the interview, and you will need to think carefully about how to ask those questions in the most productive way. You also need to think about the ethical implications of asking people to share stories that may be private or painful for them. The Canadian Oral History Association (COHA) provides a range of resources for both beginners and professional oral historians, including a list of references for further reading. You can find the COHA's website at **www.canoha.ca**. Some universities and colleges have strict rules about the use of human subjects in historical and other kinds of research, and you may be required to obtain special permission to conduct interviews, to have the questions you plan to ask approved in advance, or to arrange for special consent forms to be signed by the people you interview.

1.7 STATISTICS

Statistical data can provide invaluable insights for the historian. Statistical information generated in the past—such as the results of opinion polls or census data—can be an extremely useful primary source. When analyzing this kind of data, however, we need to remember that statistics do not necessarily provide a more accurate or reliable view of the past than any other kind of primary source. When approaching statistical material, we need to ask the same kinds of questions that we ask of other sources: Who collected the data? What kinds of questions were asked? What kinds of assumptions are embedded in the categories used to analyze the data?

Secondary sources also make extensive use of statistical information. Many historical developments—like shifts in the birthrate or changes in per capita income—can be conveyed most clearly and effectively through a table or a graph. The information in a table or a graph, of course, can be collected, presented, and interpreted in many different ways. Statistical information is as much a matter for debate among historians as any other kind of historical evidence.

A wide range of statistical data relevant to Canada and its recent history can be found on Statistics Canada's website, at **www.statscan.ca**. There you will find statistics on things like Canada's population, its gross national product, unemployment rates, resources, and demographics. Statistics Canada also makes its data sources very clear and explains its calculation methods fully. This kind of information about sources and methods is critical because it allows readers to evaluate the accuracy of the statistics. In addition, the Statistics Canada website provides links to dozens of international statistical resources.

FOR EXAMPLE: The table on the next page collates information from a century and a half of Canadian census information. In order to make sense of this information, we would need to know how the information was collected, as well as who was counted (and not counted). Have the categories or the criteria used changed over time? For example, the first census of British Columbia and Manitoba only took place in 1870, so any claims about changes in population between 1851 and 1871 would have to take that into account. While tables like these seem very precise and accurate, we also need to remember that they are based on data collected and interpreted by human beings, data that may be incomplete or imperfect. Tables based on census data highlight or summarize specific kinds of information; as historians develop new questions it is often necessary to go back to the original documents to look for new patterns.

FOR EXAMPLE: On page 21 is a sheet from the enumerator's returns for Union District on Vancouver Island in British Columbia. In 1911, this region—directly east across the island from the place where Captain Cook and his men had landed over a century earlier—was largely populated by Chinese immigrant labourers. Here, the information is much fuller and richer than in the table on the next page, but at the same

Population and Growth Components (1851–2001 Censuses)

Period	Census population at the end of period	Total population growth	Births	Deaths (thousands)	Immigration	Emigration
1851-1861	3,230	793	1,281	670	352	170
1861-1871	3,689	459	1,370	760	260	410
1871-1881	4,325	636	1,480	790	350	404
1881-1891	4,833	508	1,524	870	680	826
1891-1901	5,371	538	1,548	880	250	380
1901-1911	7,207	1,836	1,925	900	1,550	740
1911-1921	8,788	1,581	2,340	1,070	1,400	1,089
1921-1931	10,377	1,589	2,415	1,055	1,200	970
1931-1941	11,507	1,130	2,294	1,072	149	241
1941-1951	13,648	2,141	3,186	1,214	548	379
1951-1956	16,081	2,433	2,106	633	783	185
1956-1961	18,238	2,157	2,362	687	760	278
1961-1966	20,015	1,777	2,249	731	539	280
1966-1971	21,568	1,553	1,856	766	890	427
1971-1976	23,450	1,488	1,760	824	1,053	358
1976-1981	24,820	1,371	1,820	843	771	278
1981-1986	26,101	1,281	1,872	885	678	278
1986-1991	28,031	1,930	1,933	946	1,164	213
1991-1996	29,611	1,580	1,936	1,024	1,118	338
1996-2001	31,021	1,410	1,705	1,089	1,217	376

Adapted from Statistics Canada, "Population and Growth Components (1851–2001 Censuses)," http://www40.statcan.ca/l01/cst01/demo03.htm

Numbered in the Order of Visitation		Name of each person in family, household or institution	Place of habitation (Township, parish, city, town or village. Range or concession & lot or cadastral number if in town or parish, street or house number if in city, town or village. Or other description.)	Sex	Relationship to head of family or household	Single, married, widowed, divorced or legally separated	Month of birth	Year of birth	Age at last birthday	Country or place of birth (If in Canada, specify province or territory)	Year of immigration to Canada, if an immigrant	Year of naturalization, if formerly an alien	Racial or tribal origin	Nationality	Religion	Chief occupation or trade
Dwelling House	Family, household or institution															
1	2	3	4	5	6	7	8	9	10	11	12	13	14	15	16	17
	134	Wong Si To		M	Boarder	M			44	China	1901		Chinese	Chinese	Confucianism	Labourer
	134	Mock Go		M	Boarder	S			52	"	1891		"	"	"	Gardener
	135	Fung Sing		M	Head	M			44	"	1903		"	"	"	Miner
	135	Mah Fong		M	Boarder	M			36	"	1903		"	"	"	Labourer
	135	Ah Chen		M	Boarder	S			40	"	1903		"	"	"	Labourer
	135	Leon Chuck		M	Boarder	S			50	"	1895		"	"	"	Gardener
	135	Mah Hong Yen		M	Head	M			44	"	1900		"	"	"	Miner
	136	Mah Look		M	Boarder	M			25	"	1900		"	"	"	Miner
	136	Mah Him Yee		M	Boarder	M			50	"	1909		"	"	"	Labourer

Fifth Census of Canada, 1911. British Columbia, District No. 8 Comox-Atlin, Enumeration District No. 11 Union District, p. 38. http://data2.collectionscanada.ca/1911a/e078/e001935715.pdf. Library and Archives Canada.

time it is more difficult to trace broader patterns. The text itself is also difficult to read, and even the transcription provided by Census Canada, which captures much of the key information, has to leave some entries blank because they are unreadable. Even so, we can begin to draw some important conclusions. We can see that Wong Si To, the man listed in the first entry, is married but living (without his family) as a boarder in the home of Fung Sing, who is listed as the head of the household. Wong Si To's experience is typical of the people enumerated here—all of them are men, most of them are boarders, and all of them are identified as "Chinese." This would allow us to conclude that the Chinese labouring population at this time was largely if not exclusively male, and that living arrangements were dominated by boarding or lodging houses rather than family-based households. In order to understand the full significance of this information we would need to have a larger context to compare it to, which is where tables like the one on page 20 are useful. The kinds of questions you want to ask would dictate which of the two kinds of information—or what combination of them—would be most useful to you.

1.8 MAPS

Like tables of statistics, maps can be either primary or secondary sources. Historians may produce maps to convey information about the use of space or the understanding of space in different cultures. Patterns of settlement or migration, for example, can often be captured more clearly and effectively in a historical map than in a written description. Maps are also historical artifacts, and can be interpreted in the same ways that we interpret visual or written materials. Not all cultures make or value maps, and different cultures map landscapes and geography in very different ways. Maps are therefore historical documents that can tell us a great deal about the societies that produced them.

FOR EXAMPLE: The desire—and the ability—to draw accurate "world maps" was linked not only to the history of science but also to the history of European imperialism. The map on the next page, which was produced out of the same series of voyages that produced John Webber's "A View of the Habitations in Nootka Sound" (see section 1.4), reveals both the extent of the geographical knowledge that Cook and his crew produced and the curious gaps in that knowledge. (Note, for example, the lack of detailed knowledge about the west coast of North America and the south coast of Australia.) The map draws clear distinctions between different regions of the world (on coloured versions

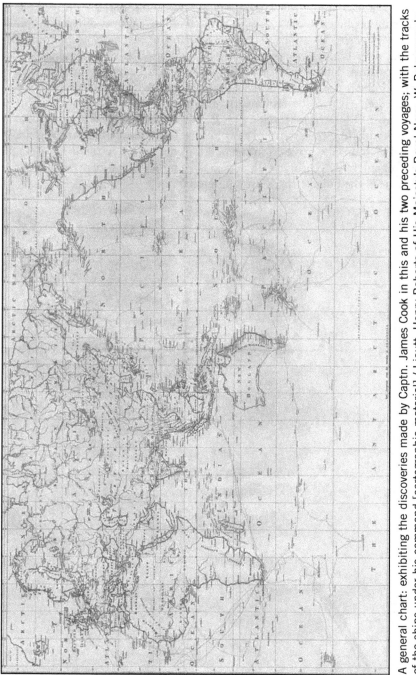

A general chart: exhibiting the discoveries made by Captn. James Cook in this and his two preceding voyages; with the tracks of the ships under his command [cartographic material] / Lieutt. Henry Roberts of His Majesty's Royal Navy; W. Palmer sculp. (London: Printed by W. and A. Strahan, for G. Nicol, & T. Cadell, 1784). Reprinted by permission of the University of British Columbia Library, Rare Books and Special Collections.

of the map, for example, Africa and the Americas were coloured green, Europe and Scandinavia in red, and Asia and Australia in yellow) reflecting eighteenth-century assumptions about cultural difference and similarity across the globe. The displacement of Europe from the centre of the map is not only a practical consideration (the mapmaker was perhaps most interested in the new information being gathered in that part of the world) but also suggests the central importance that the mapmaker gave to the regions of the Pacific that Cook's voyages had "discovered," as the map's title puts it, suggesting that these regions were unknown before the arrival of Europeans. The multiple lines tracing the "tracks" of Cook's voyages in the South Pacific reflected the belief—one that dated back centuries—that a great southern continent existed to "balance" the bulk of the Eurasian landmass.

Chapter 2

Common Writing Assignments in History: Purposes and Aims

Mary Wollstonecraft by John Opie, circa 1797
© National Portrait Gallery, London

INTRODUCTION

History students are given a variety of different writing assignments. Before we focus on the fundamentals of the research essay in Chapter 3, we will look at other common history writing assignments. Your instructor will provide directions for each assignment, and his or her grading criteria may be unique, so pay close attention to those instructions. Ask for clarification if you are unsure of the requirements. In general, however, your assignments are likely to fall into one of the categories described below.

2.1 JOURNAL ENTRIES/READING RESPONSES

Journal entries are probably the least formal kind of writing you will be asked to do in a history course. Keeping a written journal is one way for you to record your reactions to the readings in a course, and rereading your journal will give you a new perspective on the way that your responses to the material have changed over time. A journal can be a powerful resource when you review for the final examination. Reading it will also allow your professor to see whether or not you understand the books and articles she or he has assigned. Just because a journal entry is a relatively informal exercise does not mean that you should not take it seriously. A series of entries written at the end of term, based on half-remembered books and articles, may satisfy the requirements of the assignment, but it is unlikely to improve your understanding of the material.

Your professor may hand out guidelines for journal writing. If so, read them carefully and make sure that your entries include all the required elements. In general, a good journal entry should provide a short summary of the author's argument (see section 2.2), along with a brief discussion of the debates in which the author is engaging and the position he or she takes on these debates. You may also want to include your own assessment of the validity of the author's argument. Instructors often expect to see more than just the completion of assigned readings—they also expect to see you respond to some of the issues that the readings raise.

FOR EXAMPLE: The reading you have been assigned is a chapter from Barbara Taylor's study of Mary Wollstonecraft. The chapter, entitled "For the Love of God," appears in *Mary Wollstonecraft and the Feminist Imagination* (Cambridge: Cambridge University Press, 2003). The notes that follow are written in response to the first few pages of that chapter.

Notes on Taylor, "For the Love of God"

Taylor begins by pointing out that Mary Wollstonecraft came from a family without a strong religious tradition and that Wollstonecraft herself left the church relatively early in her career. But, she argues, religion was still important to her. Wollstonecraft's earliest biographers, however (including her husband, the radical William Godwin), downplayed her religious convictions. Taylor is not defending Wollstonecraft's religious beliefs—she describes herself as "impious" and one of the characters in Wollstonecraft's novel as an "irritating little saint" (p. 98)—but she does go on to emphasize the ways that Christianity could be empowering for women, and she makes it clear that we have to understand Wollstonecraft as part of that tradition. This strikes me as unusual, because much of what I have read about the history of feminism tends to be critical of religion and to see it as contributing to women's oppression, not as a form of liberation.

2.2 SUMMARIES OF READINGS

A summary (sometimes called a *précis* or an *abstract*) captures the author's main argument and ideas—it is a shorter version that provides only the essential points. A summary puts into your own words a passage from a primary or a secondary source. Ideally, a summary should be significantly shorter than the original text. Often, instructors ask their students to write chapter summaries of the readings from their course texts or source documents, which then become useful resources when reviewing the material prior to an exam. Keep in mind that, when summarizing an assigned passage, you are not being asked to rewrite it word-by-word; you are being asked to identify and compile its central or most important claims. The key to writing a successful summary is to pay close attention to what is actually on the page, and to capture the author's points concisely. Do not include things you assume should be there based on what you know about the author, and do not bring in material from other texts or from the course lectures. You should also be careful not to add your own commentary. The summary should give the reader a brief and accurate account of the passage, and readers should be able to understand it without having read the original.

2.3 PRIMARY SOURCE OR DOCUMENT ANALYSIS

As we noted above, the analysis of primary sources is one of the basic building blocks of historical writing. There is more information on reading sources in section 3.3, but here we want to emphasize a few of the key elements in a primary source analysis that make it different from other kinds of historical writing. When your instructor asks you to analyze a primary source, he or she is giving you an opportunity to "do history." The point of the exercise is not merely to have you summarize what other historians have written about this source, but to produce your own analysis of the material. If you do consult additional secondary sources for this kind of assignment, you should make very clear the distinctions between your ideas and those of other historians. One of the things that students often find frustrating about this sort of assignment is that the number of possible conclusions that can be drawn seem so limited. You might want to ask, for example, about European encounters with the Indigenous peoples of North America in the years after contact. A primary source analysis, however, forces you to focus on a passage from only one document.

███████ **FOR EXAMPLE:** You might look at the Englishman Gilbert Malcolm Sproat's account of his encounters with the Nuu-chah-nulth of British Columbia, *Scenes and Studies of Savage Life*, which was published in London in 1868.[4] In a document analysis, the focus of your study is inevitably narrowed, from "Europe" to "England," from "the Indigenous peoples of North America" to one community on the west coast of Vancouver Island, and from "the years after contact" to "the mid- to late nineteenth century." Sproat's account is an important one, but it is only one man's story, not necessarily representative of "English" attitudes more generally. It is also not a straightforward account of "what really happened" in this encounter. It clearly provides only one perspective (the perspective of the colonizer) and is limited by that perspective (you might note the reference to "savages" in Sproat's title as an indication of his attitude). That is not to say that the work has no value for historians. It may be only one small piece of evidence, but if it is read and analyzed carefully, it can still contribute to answering the broader question about European encounters with Indigenous peoples.

███████ 2.4 BIBLIOGRAPHIC ESSAYS

Every research essay should include a bibliography, which is the list of sources that were consulted and cited in the process of researching and writing the essay. A bibliographic essay is often assigned as the first stage in a research paper, and it is an opportunity for you to identify the key primary and/or secondary sources for your project. In most cases, you will be asked to provide a list of the material you plan to use in your paper. Each reference should be given in the proper format, followed by an "annotation," or short commentary, that provides a brief summary of the work (see section 2.2), and an evaluation of the contribution it will make to your study. Read each piece carefully and decide how important it is to your project. A good annotation is generally a concise paragraph that summarizes the topic of each source, its main themes or arguments, and its usefulness to your research project. If you have consulted many sources, it may be helpful to organize your bibliography into separate lists, giving primary sources first and then secondary sources.

███████ 2.5 BOOK REVIEWS

Professional historians rely on published book reviews to learn about new sources available in their field. A good book review provides a brief summary of the work, a discussion of its strengths and weaknesses, and

---

[4] Gilbert Malcolm Sproat, *Scenes and Studies of Savage Life* (London: Smith, Elder, 1868).

an evaluation of its contribution to the field. Although a reviewer may mention whether or not a book is well written or accessible to a broad audience, these are not normally the central concerns of a book review in history. Historical monographs are not novels, and they are not intended primarily to entertain, although some of the best work does manage to accomplish that. One good way to open a review is to begin by introducing the author or editor and explaining why the book was written—an important theme that authors usually discuss in their introductions. After describing the sources on which the book is based and summarizing the book's principal claims and conclusions, you should discuss whether the author has supported his or her claims, and whether the source is useful or not. You could also mention any supporting materials in the book, such as photographs, charts, maps, and diagrams. Your review should focus on the contributions the work makes to the debates and issues in the field, as you have probably discussed in class. You can find examples of professionally written book reviews in most historical journals. The *Canadian Journal of History*, *Histoire sociale/Social History*, and *The Canadian Historical Review* all publish book reviews regularly. Consult these journals, or others recommended by your instructor, for models.

Sometimes, you may be asked to write a *comparative* book review. In this case, you are assigned (or asked to choose) two books that deal with similar or related themes.

FOR EXAMPLE: You have been asked to write a comparative review of the following two books:

Tennant, Paul M. *Aboriginal Peoples and Politics: The Indian Land Question in British Columbia, 1849–1989*. Vancouver: University of British Columbia Press, 1990.

Tough, Frank. *'As Their Natural Resources Fail': Native Peoples and the Economic History of Northern Manitoba, 1870–1930*. Vancouver: University of British Columbia Press, 1996.

A comparative book review could highlight differences in focus and subject:

> Both of these books deal with related, though not identical, themes. Paul Tennant's work focuses on British Columbia, while Frank Tough deals with the situation in Manitoba. Tennant's work covers a longer time span than Tough's. Tennant's work is directly focused on the land claims issue, while Tough's discussion of Aboriginal title is only one part of a broader history of Aboriginal peoples and their interactions with both the Crown and the Hudson's Bay Company.

A comparative book review might also explore the authors' different approaches to history:

> While both of these books deal with the history of Native–newcomer relations, neither author is a "historian" in the narrow sense: Paul Tennant is a political scientist, and Frank Tough trained as a cultural geographer and is now Director of a Native Studies program. Paul Tennant's approach is primarily chronological and descriptive. His overall aim is to "reveal something of the remarkable achievements of the Indian peoples in their steadfast pursuit of their land rights through peaceful political means" (p. ix). Tough, in contrast, criticizes the chronological approach explicitly and instead adopts a thematic and materialist approach that attempts to combine "economic history with the geography of treaty and Aboriginal rights" (p. 13). On the other hand, both authors reject what might be described as postmodern approaches to First Nations history.

A comparative book review is not expected to deal with all of the issues raised in both works. Choose the themes or areas of agreement or disagreement that you think are the most important and focus on those. An in-depth and detailed study of a few well-chosen issues will be more effective than a superficial survey of a very large number of different points.

2.6 HISTORIOGRAPHICAL PAPERS

The word "historiography" means literally "writing about history." You might think of it as a "map" that lays out the landscape or the geography of writing about a particular historical topic. A historiographical essay focuses not on what happened but on how historians *have written about* what happened. It is a self-conscious reflection on how we do history, and on how the writing about historical issues, people, or events has changed over time. This kind of paper explores the questions we ask as historians, the methods we employ, and the areas of debate within a particular field. You can think of it as an expansion of the comparative book review because it usually reviews a series of articles and books grouped together around a central theme.

For example, the debate over the European "discovery" of the Americas has been transformed over the last generation, and these historical arguments came to public attention in the 1990s as a result of debates over the commemoration of Christopher Columbus' voyage to the so-called "New World" in 1492. A number of historians have now reassessed the historical impact of the encounter between natives and newcomers, working to uncover native peoples' perspective on these events. Here we can see a clear historiographical turning point, and a shift in the direction of the historical debate. A good historiographical essay takes note of such developments in order to make the point that the way we think about this issue has changed and developed over time.

It is important, however, to make sure that a historiographical essay does not read like a series of separate book reviews strung together. Use your discussion of the individual books and articles to develop different aspects of the argument you make in your paper. Think about the kinds of themes and questions discussed above, in the section on comparative book reviews. What are the major points of agreement and disagreement in the books and articles you have read? Has the focus of the debate changed over time? Can you trace the development of new questions or the impact of new approaches? Remember that you are developing an *argument about* the material in this field, not simply providing a description of the material.

Sometimes you will be asked to write a short paper on only one article or a chapter in a book. This kind of assignment—which might also be described as a "critical commentary" or "secondary source analysis"—is more formal than a "reading response" or journal entry, but it does not require you to do as much research as a book review or a historiographical paper. In this kind of assignment you should be thinking about the same kinds of questions that we have outlined above, in our discussion of book reviews and historiographical papers. Here too, you need to make sure that your paper makes an argument about the material you have read. What contribution does the piece make to historical debates? What kinds of evidence has the author used? How convincing are the authors' claims? Remember that these kinds of short papers are no less challenging than longer papers. In fact, shorter papers are often more difficult as you have to make every word count.

2.7 EXAMS: WRITING EFFECTIVE SHORT ANSWERS AND ESSAY QUESTION ANSWERS

Examinations are usually written under pressure and in a limited amount of time, so they are not expected to be as polished or as sophisticated as the take-home papers we will be discussing below. An ideal exam answer, however, still has many of the same elements that are found in more formal essays. Before you begin answering questions on an examination, however, you should take a few moments to think about your strategy. Read the whole examination paper carefully before you begin answering any of the questions. Look at the breakdown of marks for the different sections. If one section is worth half of the grade for the whole examination, then plan on spending half of your time on that section. Read the instructions carefully to make sure you are addressing the question that your instructor has posed. If the question has a number of different parts, make sure that your answer addresses each part appropriately. Here we will discuss a few types of questions common to history exams.

"Short answer" questions usually ask you to write only a short paragraph. For example, a common form of short answer question asks you to "identify and explain the significance of" a person, place, or thing, and many students have difficulty answering this kind of question correctly. When drafting your answer, you should not only provide the factual information that satisfies the "identification" part of the question, but also make a case for its significance by linking it to the larger themes discussed in your course.

FOR EXAMPLE: "Identify and explain the significance of: *Sputnik*" (three points)

Ineffective Answer

Sputnik was a satellite that the Soviets launched that beat the United States into orbit. It went around the world many times but then fell down to earth. It was a big part of the space race.

This answer is too brief, provides limited detail, and only hints at the significance of the launch. This answer would deserve no more than one point out of three.

Better Answer

Sputnik was a satellite launched into orbit by the Soviet Union in 1957. It broadcast a radio signal back to earth. The launch frightened the United States because America hadn't yet launched any similar satellites. The Sputnik scare was a big part of the Cold War.

This answer provides further detail, and outlines the significance of the launch in a bit more depth, but still does not fully address the question of why the launch of Sputnik was such an important event. This answer would deserve no more than two points.

👍👍 Effective Answer

Sputnik was a satellite launched into earth orbit by the Soviet Union in October 1957, beating the American Vanguard rocket program. This caused a panic in the U.S. and Western Europe because the rocket that launched Sputnik could also launch an atomic weapon at America. The launch of Sputnik triggered the Space Race between the U.S. and the U.S.S.R., which was a big part of the Cold War and the race to build up stocks of nuclear missiles.

This answer identifies the term *Sputnik* in sufficient detail before moving on to address the significance of the launch in depth. It explains precisely *why* the launch caused panic in the West, and what the long-term *consequences* of the launch meant for the Cold War. This answer would deserve three points. Note also that the strongest answer is not much longer than the previous ones. It is concise and dense, discussing more than one concept in each sentence. This is an efficient use of time, which is critical when writing exams.

When writing a response to a longer essay-style question, it is equally important to make an argument and not just provide a list of information. First of all, read the question carefully, and look for clues in the formulation of the question that will help you in developing your answer. If the question starts with a statement and asks you to "comment" on or "discuss" the claim, then you know that you are being asked to take a position on a historical problem or debate. Next, take the time to plan your answer and support the general claims you make with specific examples from the course material. If your instructor has been emphasizing the importance of historical debates throughout the course, then that can be a very useful starting point for thinking about the argument you want to make. Planning the essay is also an excellent way to make sure that you give yourself enough time to complete the exam, as it will give you a sense of how quickly you need to move through your various points to finish in the time allowed. You can begin by jotting down a quick outline of the answer you plan to write, and then following it as you expand upon each point. When you begin writing your answer, avoid rewriting the question at the outset, unless you are asked specifically to do so. This wastes valuable time that can be better spent formulating your claim, or the point of your answer, in order to let the reader know where you are headed.

▆▆▆ FOR EXAMPLE: This question gives you an opportunity to agree or to disagree with its opening claim: "Without the political imperatives of the Cold War, the United States would not have entered the 'space race.' Discuss."

In this case, there is no one "right" answer. A well-argued case, supported by appropriate evidence, could be made on either side. If the question asks you to list a series of causes or consequences, to analyze a passage or an image, or to identify an event or a person, then you would want to take a different approach. The most important thing is to make sure that your answer relates to the question in a direct, meaningful way.

▆▆▆ 2.8 RESEARCH PROPOSALS

Your instructor may ask you to provide a short research proposal as a first step in writing an essay. This is often the case when you are required to do original research based on primary sources. Writing a research proposal can be a tricky exercise, as you are being asked to write about a paper you hope to write based on research that you have not yet completed. The research proposal is an opportunity for you to develop a series of historical questions and to identify the sources that will enable you to answer those questions.

To develop effective historical questions, you need to familiarize yourself with some of the recent secondary source material on your topic. Ask the kinds of questions we outlined in section 2.6, on historiographical papers. Look for the major points of agreement and disagreement in the field. What questions remain to be answered? What hypotheses remain to be proved or disproved? How might the conclusions reached by the authors you have read be challenged, extended, or revised? The answers to these questions are the starting point for your research. The next step is to find a source or set of sources that will enable you to answer the questions you have posed. Sometimes (as we saw in the discussion of primary source or document analysis in section 2.3), you need to narrow down broad questions in order to make them manageable, to ensure that you can answer them with the resources you have available. At the same time, remember that historical research is not always predictable, and it does not always proceed according to plan. Sometimes, you will find that a research project begins with a source or set of sources that you find puzzling or intriguing—a collection of family letters, a run of old magazines or trade journals, or a box of faded photographs. If you are working at an institution with limited library resources, you may also find that it is more practical to begin by locating sources that relate to a topic that you are interested in. Essentially, your task is to become familiar enough with the historiography to develop an argument about your sources, one that will allow you to make a contribution to a larger debate.

Once you have identified worthwhile sources and appropriate research questions, it is time to draft a proposal that draws them all together. Your instructor will issue specific guidelines on the format this should take, but here are some general tips on how to approach it. You should begin by outlining your topic. Describe its importance and discuss your sources, both primary and secondary, in detail. Summarize the sorts of historical debates that authors have been having about the subject. (This brief discussion of the existing secondary sources is known as a literature review.) Finally, introduce and discuss your proposed research questions along with any preliminary conclusions or expectations that you have drawn. These can later be developed into the central argument, or thesis, of your essay. Of course, your final conclusions may contrast sharply with your initial expectations. This is one of the things that characterizes good research. Just as a police officer investigating a crime may have to change hypotheses as she or he uncovers new evidence, you should also be prepared to discover unexpected and interesting results as you proceed with your research.

2.9 RESEARCH ESSAYS

The process of researching, organizing, and preparing a research essay is similar to the prosecution of a case before a jury of one's peers in a court of law. Popular television "courtroom dramas" have familiarized many of us with the techniques used to assemble a criminal case and present it in court. These techniques are therefore useful analogies when describing the various steps in writing a research essay. A case must be investigated, evidence must be collected, weighed, and organized, and a clearly articulated argument must be presented to an audience that will ultimately decide the merits of the author's case. We will develop this analogy in more detail in the next chapter.

A good research paper combines elements of many of the different kinds of papers that we have discussed in this chapter. In a paper that asks you to do some original research, such as a major term paper using primary sources or an honours thesis, you would begin by identifying the key texts you plan to examine and developing your own annotated bibliography. The paper itself should include a discussion of historical debates in the field you are writing about, as well as an analysis of the primary sources on which you are basing your argument. Because the research essay is such an important element of history courses, we devote the next chapter to a detailed examination of this form of writing.

Research Essays: The Writing Process from Start to Finish

A young Mao Zedong, Yan'an, 1938
Collection J. A. Fox/Magnum Photos

INTRODUCTION

This chapter, on writing research essays, is the heart of our guide. Even though research essays are a crucial part of most history courses, students are rarely taught *how* to write them. Here we break down the process of writing a historical research essay into its component parts. To tackle a research essay assignment, you first need to conduct a thorough investigation and make appropriate research notes, then plan and write your first draft in stages. The first draft is only the beginning; a good paper gets rewritten and edited, often more than once, before it is handed in. In this chapter, we will show you not just how to write a research essay in history, but how to do it well.

In our discussion of the writing process, we have illustrated our points with "quotations" from four Sample Essays. You have already encountered themes from some of these essays in earlier sections of this guide. As we discuss how to draft a useful introduction or how to write an effective thesis statement, we will provide examples from one of these four imaginary essays. We hope that the contrast between the various examples will allow you to see the difference between effective and ineffective elements of research essays.

A) INTRODUCING THE FOUR SAMPLE ESSAYS

Essay 1: "Technological Innovation and the Apollo Program" is an example of a *research essay* that might be written for a course on world history or the history of technology. Your instructor has asked you to look at the role of science and technology in the post–Second World War era, and you have chosen to explore the role of computers in the "space race" of the 1960s.

Essay 2: "Nature, Reason and Equality in Mary Wollstonecraft's *A Vindication of the Rights of Woman*" is an example of a *primary source* or *document analysis*, written for a course on modern European history. Your assignment asks you to choose a non-fiction text published between 1750 and 1850 and to analyze the arguments it makes about one of the political controversies of the time.

Essay 3: "Stories of Contact: Debates in First Nations' History" is a *historiographical* paper, and it asks you to explore a *historical debate*—to take a stand for or against a particular position. This example could come from a paper written for a Canadian history or First Nations' history course. In this case, you are asked to write on the following topic: "According to Jennifer Brown and Elizabeth Vibert, 'it has become a central tenet of colonial studies that in representing their encounters with indigenous peoples, Euro-Americans were writing about themselves as much as they were writing about others.'[5] Discuss."

Essay 4: "The Origins of Communist China: Mao Zedong and the War of Resistance against Japan, 1937–45" is the sort of *research essay* that might be written for a course on the history of international relations or the history of the Cold War. Your instructor has asked you to analyze a twentieth-century ideological struggle, and you have chosen to focus on the agenda of the Chinese Communist leadership during its fight against Japan during the Second World War (known as China's War of Resistance) and how that struggle enabled the Communists to later win the Chinese Civil War in 1949.

Notice that each of these essays expects you to take a *position*—to make an argument about the topic. There is no one right answer to any of the questions posed in the Sample Essays, but all of them require you

---

[5] Brown and Vibert, "Introduction," *Reading Beyond Words*, xiii.

to take a stand. In Essays 1 and 4 you have to make an argument about how and why a particular set of historical events unfolded. In Essay 2, you have to make an argument about Mary Wollstonecraft's views of women and women's rights, and in Essay 3 you have to decide whether you agree or disagree with Brown and Vibert. The essay writer, like the prosecutor in a trial, aims to present a convincing case. Like a criminal case, a research essay must be well researched, organized, and prepared, and it must be presented logically and coherently. It must also support its claims with convincing evidence. Most importantly, it makes an argument—like a claim about the guilt or innocence of the person on trial. Remember as well that you are making your argument to a particular audience. You are presenting your case to a judge (your instructor) and a jury composed of your classmates, who are your peers. As we proceed through the steps involved in researching and writing your paper, we will reflect on the equivalent challenges faced by a prosecutor, who is obligated to support the argument, or charges, that she or he has made.

3.1 CHOOSING A TOPIC

Students often have difficulty choosing a topic because of the wide variety of possible subjects. Some instructors issue a list of suggested topics, but you are often free to consider another topic as long as you obtain the instructor's permission. When choosing a topic, consider the following:

- *Above all, what interests you?* Review the instructor's lectures, the assigned texts, and any supporting course materials. World history courses are often very broad in their coverage, but there will undoubtedly be several subject areas that interest you. Often, a good place to start is by focusing on the history of a country or region that you would like to visit. Or, you could explore the historical roots of an issue that engages you today, whether that is the history of student activism, of shopping, or of football. Speak to your instructor or teaching assistant if you have difficulty choosing a topic.

- *Is the topic manageable?* If it is too broad, the instructor may recommend that you narrow down your investigation to make it more appropriate to the length of the paper assigned. Like a criminal case that is too large to be handled in a single trial, broad historical topics such as "the position of women in Europe" should be focused more carefully, in order to determine which aspect or aspects of the topic can be argued effectively in the space available.

- *Is there adequate source material available?* Sometimes, the question you want to ask is simply unanswerable with the resources to which you have access. For example, you might want to know how the Indigenous people portrayed in the image we discussed in section 1.4, on visual sources, perceived Cook and his companions (see page 14.) While historians and scholars working in First Nations history have developed many innovative techniques to try to answer this question, especially through the use of oral histories, you may not have access to the kind of material that would provide the Indigenous perspective on this encounter.[6] This is still a very good question to ask, but you may need to reformulate it in order to be able to take advantage of the resources that are available. No lawyer would prosecute a case if there was insufficient evidence to support the charges.

- *Is the topic a historical one?* You should be careful to avoid sensationalist topics; instead, focus on topics that can be dealt with historically. For example, where a theologian might ask, "Does God exist?" or a scientist might ask, "How can the development of the universe be explained without invoking the concept of God?" the historian asks very different questions: "How did belief (or disbelief) in God shape the actions of this particular person or group?" or "How did new scientific ideas affect religious institutions in this particular time and place?" Finding an angle of historical inquiry often involves asking how and why particular events or circumstances influenced individuals and their societies.

Sometimes, your instructor may provide you with a very focused question, which asks you to deal with a specific text or issue. In other cases, however, the question you are given may be very broad. In Essay 2, you can choose any European text dealing with a political issue published over a hundred-year period. There are literally hundreds of different topics that you could choose for a paper like this.

FOR EXAMPLE: In the discussion of primary source or document analysis (section 2.3), we talked about the ways that an interest in the encounter between European and Indigenous peoples needs to be refined to produce a manageable topic. In the case of Essay 2, you are again being forced to make a series of choices about how you want to

---

[6] See Clayton, "Captain Cook," for an example of this kind of scholarship.

focus your paper. The sample paper discussed here focuses on a specific political issue (the rights of women) at a particular moment (the late eighteenth century) in one country (England). The text we have selected is *A Vindication of the Rights of Woman*, written at the time of the French Revolution by the English feminist Mary Wollstonecraft. The book, which was published in 1792, was written to take advantage of contemporary excitement over political events in France.[7]

This would be a good text to choose if you are interested in the history of women and gender or in the history of feminist political movements. If you are more interested in labour history or the history of colonialism or of education, then you could choose texts dealing with those issues. In each case, however, you need to think about the issues we have raised here: Is the topic manageable? Are the relevant sources available? Can it be dealt with historically? And, most important of all, do you find it interesting?

3.2 DEVELOPING QUESTIONS AND RESEARCHING YOUR PAPER

Once you have settled on an appropriate and interesting topic, it is time to become more familiar with the literature on the subject and to assemble the evidence that you will present when arguing your case. Once you have a general idea of the topic that you wish to explore, this phase of the research process resembles a police investigation. At this point, you are developing a series of questions and some tentative hypotheses, but you are not yet in a position to draw any firm conclusions. The kinds of questions and hypotheses you develop will depend on your topic, but some general guidelines apply. Your course textbook is a good place to start. Textbooks give the "big picture" and inevitably simplify the material they present. They also represent the state of the field at the time that they were published, and new studies (like yours) can help to refine and revise those earlier claims.

Start early and you will have much greater success finding what you are looking for. Even the best university library's resources are placed under considerable strain when the end of term approaches, as hundreds of students begin working on research essays at the same time. You may find that your topic was more popular than you realized; if you delay too long, all of the most useful materials may already be in use. Start by

---

[7] Mary Wollstonecraft, *A Vindication of the Rights of Woman: With Strictures on Political and Moral Subjects* in *The Vindications: The Rights of Men and The Rights of Woman*, ed. D. L. Macdonald and Kathleen Scherf (1792; Peterborough, ON: Broadview Press, 1997).

examining the library's catalogue and take notes to keep track of what you discover. Most libraries also provide access to electronic catalogues and databases, and you may even find that you are able to download useful resources directly from the Internet. (See the discussion in Chapter 1 on using search engines in historical research.) Remember to use the appropriate keywords as you search—check your textbook, course readings, and lecture notes to see what kinds of terms historians have used to discuss the topics you are interested in. Examine authors' bibliographies for further sources. Once you have identified a series of questions that you hope your research will answer, your next step is to develop a list of relevant primary and secondary sources. If you find a particularly valuable secondary source, the author or authors will have listed their own sources for your information. The citation of sources is a fundamental part of history as a discipline, so other writers' bibliographies will give you many titles for additional reading. Some may be very obscure primary sources, or even private interviews and manuscripts, but more common secondary sources will often be found in most college and university libraries. Read these bibliographies carefully. They often provide valuable clues to the most important or controversial works in a particular field. If a potentially valuable source is on loan, you can recall it or request that it be held for you when another patron returns it. In addition, if you find titles for sources not available in your university's library, you can request that they be ordered and delivered via interlibrary loan.

Approach the research for your paper with an open mind. Be careful not to make assumptions about what you will find based on your own beliefs or preconceived notions about the past. Making unexpected connections is an exciting element of historical research. You should start by developing a list of questions that you hope to answer. At the beginning, your questions may be very broad and general, but as you go along, you should find that your questions not only become more focused but also more challenging.

FOR EXAMPLE: If you were working on Essay 2, you might start with a few basic questions, such as "How does Wollstonecraft characterize the position of women in her society? What kinds of subjects does she cover?" These are relatively easy questions to answer; if you stop there, you will probably find yourself writing a fairly straightforward summary of Wollstonecraft's text. (See section 3.3, on reading sources, for tips on developing more sophisticated questions about your material.) You may discover that the questions you started with are unanswerable. That does not necessarily mean that they were not good questions, but it may mean that you will have to find another way to get at the answers. Talk to your instructor if you find yourself in this position. Many historians have faced the same kinds of problems, and you may be able to benefit from their experiences.

As you do your research, it is crucial that you take careful notes. We cannot overemphasize the importance of taking notes and keeping track of your findings during the investigative phase of your writing assignment. This activity is the equivalent of building a case file for the defence of your argument. Some sources cover a long period or a diverse series of topics. Each individual part or chapter of a monograph or an edited volume may have its own argument and may draw a series of specific conclusions. As you read, keep track of the "big picture," so that you know where the author is headed. If the argument or the information appears to be irrelevant to your investigation, consider using another source instead.

Careless note-taking can result in significant errors of interpretation. (For example, if you miss a word like "not" or "never," you can completely transform the meaning of the sentence you have found.) Furthermore, it can even leave you vulnerable to a charge of plagiarism, which is a serious form of intellectual theft, if you accidentally present the words or ideas of one of your sources as your own. Always start by taking down all of the information you will need to cite the work in your notes and bibliography. (See section 4.4 for more information.) You may want to keep your notes on index cards, in a notebook, or on a computer. Whatever system you use to record your notes, make sure that you are able to retrieve information easily and accurately and that you are always able to confirm the source of that information. (Never take notes in a library book or otherwise deface your institution's resources.)

It is unlikely that you will be able to read everything ever published on the topic you have chosen. Even if you could, this is probably not necessary. If you have chosen your materials carefully, you may notice as you proceed with your research that much of what you are reading is already familiar to you. You may even begin to recognize the sources that are being referred to without having to look at the footnotes. At this point, it is a good idea to begin planning your paper and writing a first draft. As you write, you will probably discover that there are gaps in your knowledge that need to be filled by new research. If you go back to your sources at that point, you will find that you can read them much more efficiently than you could at the beginning, as you will now have a much clearer idea of the kinds of material that you need to complete your essay.

3.3 READING YOUR SOURCES

There are two principal types of historical sources—primary and secondary. In this section, we discuss how each should be used in your research. (For definitions of primary and secondary source material, see sections 1.1 and 1.2.)

A) PRIMARY SOURCES

As we noted in Chapter 1, when working with primary sources the first thing you need to do is to determine what *kind* of source you are working with. Is it propaganda? A newspaper report? Fiction? A diary or letter? Different kinds of writing employ different conventions, techniques, and vocabularies. You need to be aware of these as you read.

You should also think about the context in which the work was produced. Who wrote it? When? What were they trying to accomplish? In the case of Mary Wollstonecraft, she was writing to persuade radicals in both England and France to make women's rights an integral part of the revolutionary agenda. She was not simply describing her society but arguing a particular political case.

FOR EXAMPLE: What do we make of a passage like this, in which Wollstonecraft criticizes the women of her time for their obsessions with fashion?

> Ignorance and the mistaken cunning that nature sharpens in weak heads as a principle of self-preservation, render women very fond of dress, and produce all the vanity which such fondness may naturally be expected to generate, to the exclusion of emulation and magnanimity.[8]

Be careful not to go beyond the limits of your material—make sure your conclusions and inferences are supported by your source. While Wollstonecraft may have been right in her characterization of at least some of the women of her society, this passage does not allow us to draw that conclusion. We know only that she *argued* that the women of her day were "very fond of dress."

Wollstonecraft wrote from a particular perspective and with her own agenda. That should not lead us to dismiss her work as "biased." All sources are "biased" in some way, in that they all come from some particular perspective. That does not mean that they are valueless. They

---

[8] Wollstonecraft, 333.

SOURCES

can tell us a great deal about the kinds of perspectives that existed in past societies. In this case, Wollstonecraft's writings tell us about the way that the world looked to an educated, politically engaged woman living through a time of great political and social upheaval. A close study of her work can reveal the limits and possibilities of her worldview, and it can help us understand how basic assumptions about the relationships between men and women have (or have not) changed between her time and ours. You need to move beyond identifying the *fact* of bias to an exploration of the various ways in which Wollstonecraft's perspective shaped the way that she saw the world. It may be tempting to try to find a more "objective" source that will tell you what was "really happening" in Wollstonecraft's time. But, as we emphasized in Chapter 1, it is important to remember that such ideal, completely objective sources do not exist. Historians have to work with fragmentary, partial, and sometimes contradictory primary evidence, simply because it is often the only evidence we have available. For this reason, it is crucial to make sure that we use the evidence that we do have as well and as carefully as possible.

Reading historical sources carefully often means dealing with difficult or unfamiliar vocabulary. For example, in the passage cited above, Wollstonecraft uses phrases that are complicated and often difficult to understand; even familiar words (such as "emulation" or "magnanimity") seem to be used in unusual or unfamiliar ways. When you encounter passages like these in your research, take the time to reread them carefully, to make sure that you understand the point the author is making. Historical dictionaries, such as the *Oxford English Dictionary*—which is available either in print or online through most reference collections—can help you understand how people in the past used words or phrases differently than we do today.

When you are reading primary sources you need to read beneath the surface of the material. Trace the patterns in the author's argument, analyze their assumptions, and look for what appear to us to be contradictions or ambiguities. Be especially attentive to things that surprise or puzzle you—these may be clues to a worldview or set of assumptions that is radically different from our own.

FOR EXAMPLE: On the next page, there is a sample worksheet that might be created when researching your paper. In it, you can see the notes that the writer of the essay has taken, as well as the sorts of questions that develop through a careful review of the material. By working out your ideas as you read, rather than waiting until you sit down in front of the computer to write, you can organize your thoughts and your questions as your research develops. Later, when you are building the outline of your essay, worksheets like these can be very valuable because they can remind you not only of what you read but also of the questions that the material generated. The kind of evidence you need to support your argument is not always obvious or easy to find. You need to think carefully about the material you are reading, to work to understand its meaning and its context.

"Ignorance and the mistaken cunning that nature sharpens in weak heads as a principle of self-preservation, render women very fond of dress, and produce all the vanity which such fondness may naturally be expected to generate, to the exclusion of emulation and magnanimity." (p. 333)

"Ignorance"—starts with the assumption that women are ignorant and that they have "weak heads." (is she talking about all women here? Surely she does not include herself in this category?)

Reference to nature—suggestion that nature (human nature?) has given even the weak a desire for self-preservation—if people have "weak minds" (does that mean they are not educated?), then they will "naturally" develop "mistaken cunning" (why mistaken? What is she getting at here?)

(Note—check how she uses "nature" in other passages.)

* If women are weak-headed and ignorant, then they use whatever resources they can in order to survive—they are cunning enough to know that attention to fashion will make them popular—all that time spent on fashion will make them vain—and their vanity develops at the expense of "emulation and magnanimity." (Note—check eighteenth-century definitions of those words.)

Oxford English Dictionary—in the eighteenth century, "emulation" meant the desire to excel; "magnanimity" was generosity or nobility of spirit

* Leaving women in ignorance naturally makes women vain and leaves them obsessed with fashion, which crowds out nobler virtues.

Note—nature and virtue? Think about links.

There are a number of things to notice here. First, the note-taker doesn't assume in advance that he or she knows what Wollstonecraft believes about women, education, and fashion. You should come to your sources with questions and a provisional conceptual framework, but remember that the process of research can and even should demonstrate the limitations of our questions and categories. As historians, we need to pay careful attention to what the text actually says, using the text as evidence to test our assumptions and explanations.

B) SECONDARY SOURCES

The conclusions that we draw from the kinds of primary sources described in the previous section can then be used to confirm, amplify, revise, or challenge the claims made by the existing secondary literature. When you read the secondary literature, you should not only be looking for information about your topic—you should also be looking at the ways that different historians have approached the topic. Like a good history essay, a good historical book or article *makes a case* for something; it develops an argument *about* the material or topic.

All good historical writing has an argument. All historical scholarship is part of an ongoing debate or conversation, so historical writing always builds on and refers back to previous historical work. In most cases, the argument is introduced early in a piece of historical writing, usually in an introductory section. Sometimes, the same claim is made more clearly or strongly in a concluding section. The argument may have many different elements, but there are three elements that you need to find:

1. A statement of the current consensus in the field. Sometimes, there are a number of competing positions, and you may find a short account of one or more of them.

2. An identification of the problem with that consensus or position.

3. A proposed solution.

FOR EXAMPLE: Let's work on one of the secondary sources used in Essay 3. The assignment question actually provides you with the first element—the consensus in the field. It reads: "it has become a central tenet of colonial studies that in representing their encounters with indigenous peoples, Euro-Americans were writing about themselves as much as they were writing about others." This statement comes from the editors' introduction to a collection of essays on First Nations history. One of the first essays in that collection, Paul W. DePasquale's "'Worth the Noting': European Ambivalence and Aboriginal Agency in Meta

SOURCES

Incognita, 1576–1578," immediately challenges this claim. The author's argument develops as follows:

1. DePasquale starts by identifying the current consensus (element 1). He writes, "I recognized the various strategies that European writers used to convey their mastery in the new world."[9]

2. The very same sentence, however, also identifies a problem with that consensus (element 2). The whole sentence reads, "But while I recognized the various strategies that European writers used to convey their mastery in the new world, I could also see, through a process of reading informed by my own experiences of First Nations people, many examples of Aboriginal agency...." DePasquale argues, then, that the weakness of the current consensus is that it does not pay enough attention to the ways in which Aboriginal peoples also played a role in shaping European perceptions.

3. So, how does DePasquale propose to solve this problem (element 3)? He writes, "We need to examine critically how European encounters with Aboriginal peoples helped to shape their textual representations, as this can help us to better understand the roles of sixteenth- and seventeenth-century Native peoples."

Together, these three elements constitute the author's argument. As you summarize each of these elements, be aware of the *kind* of claims the author is making and the words you use to describe it. Phrases such as "the author *argues*," "she *recognizes*," or "he *identifies*" all convey slightly different positions. (See section 3.8 for a fuller discussion of the importance of word choice.)

Of course, historical debates change and develop over time. The consensus in 2009 is very different from the consensus in 1959; in another 10 or 20 years historians will probably have developed a range of new positions and arguments. So, if other historians reading DePasquale's work find this argument convincing, it may go on to form the basis for a new consensus. This is why it is important to be aware of publication and reprint dates of your secondary sources. Historical debate is an ongoing argument, and it is helpful to know where in this ongoing argument a particular piece fits.

Note: It is also important to distinguish between an author who is summarizing other people's views and an author who is expressing his or her own views. Historians often summarize other scholars' claims in order to critique or dispute them. You also need to be careful to distinguish between historians' own views and those of their historical subjects.

---

[9] Paul W. DePasquale, "'Worth the Noting': European Ambivalence and Aboriginal Agency in Meta Incognita, 1576–1578," in *Reading Beyond Words*, 8.

FOR EXAMPLE: Imagine that a passage in a secondary work reads, "Eighteenth-century anatomical writing was profoundly misogynistic. Women were not only physically but also mentally inferior to men." It would be inaccurate to paraphrase this by stating, "The author thinks that women are inferior to men." In fact, the author is merely assessing the beliefs held by eighteenth-century anatomical writers and is not sharing his or her own opinion on the subject.

3.4 DEVELOPING AN ARGUMENT: FORMULATING A THESIS STATEMENT

In this section, we suggest some ways you can incorporate the three elements of good historical writing that we identified above (in the section on reading secondary sources) into your own writing.

First of all, a research essay cannot simply *report* on historical events or ideas; it must have a point to make. The reader wants to know, "Why am I reading this?" "What is the author arguing here?" A prosecutor would not simply present evidence to a jury without arguing a particular case. The evidence itself does not constitute an argument; it must be presented to the reader after he or she has been advised of the argument, or "charges." Remember as well that there are always at least two sides to an argument; your claim must be something that could be disputed or debated. An obvious or uncontroversial claim—"science played a role in the 'space race'" or "Mary Wollstonecraft wrote about women"—is unlikely to make a successful essay. The most interesting debates are often those in which a strong case can be made for more than one side (see the question in Essay 3, for example, where many books and articles have been published on both sides of the argument). At the same time, you should not take the need to be controversial too far. For example, an essay that argued—against all available historical evidence—that the Communists actually lost the Chinese Civil War in 1949 would not be able to make a convincing case.

A *thesis* is the central argument or claim being made by the author. The thesis should provide the research paper with its point, the reason for presenting the evidence uncovered during the investigation of the topic. It is the "case" being made for the reader's consideration. Writing a paper without a thesis is like reviewing evidence without prosecuting a case—the reader will be confused and may even grow irritated. Imagine how you would feel if—after listening to a lawyer present hours of evidence—you were still not sure whether he or she was acting for the prosecution or the defence. An essay without a thesis would produce the same effect.

The *thesis statement*, or the statement of the author's argument, usually appears early in the paper—in the introduction, or very soon thereafter. The *introduction* presents the topic to the audience, defines the subject, period, and event or ideas to be discussed. The thesis statement usually forms part of the introduction; its special function is to make clear to the reader exactly what the author is arguing.

When formulating a thesis statement, you should consider the following questions:

- *What is it about this topic that is controversial?* Many topics are naturally problem-based and are readily debatable. Determining where you stand in a debate is a useful way to begin to formulate an argument. Are you convinced by the newer approaches to a particular topic or not? Even if you do agree with new approaches, you may feel that something important has been lost as historians have changed their questions or their focus. Other topics ask you to trace causal relationships between events. While there may be several competing schools of thought on why a particular event took place in the way it did, you may see one or two factors as primary or most important. Focusing on these and giving reasons for your choice will lead you to a thesis for your paper.

- *Are there specific themes within this topic that I can investigate?* Many historical topics—such as war or social or political revolutions—are very broad. You may wish to examine such a topic by focusing on a particular theme, such as the role of women or minorities, the state of political or gender relations, or the influence of science and technology. You can also choose to explore both causes and consequences. How did the actors or agents affect events, or how did the events affect the actors?

- *Can the evidence that I have uncovered support the claim I am making?* It is wise to consider the evidence you have found during your investigation and weigh it objectively before writing your essay. Devising an argument before reviewing all of the relevant material can lead to the unfortunate discovery that your argument is flawed or is not supportable. Working in reverse order to substantiate an uncertain argument is the equivalent of finding your suspect guilty or innocent before you see all the evidence. Read your sources critically and take careful notes of what you have discovered. These notes will become crucial to the formulation of your thesis, or case. After you have formulated an argument, these notes will help form the body of your essay. The more notes you have, and the more carefully you have

THESIS

kept track of the key evidence you have uncovered, the more easily you will be able to construct and link together the main points of your paper.

The broader your topic, the more likely it is that your paper will be able to deal with it only superficially. In section 3.2, on conducting research, we talked about the need to develop questions that can guide your research. As we noted there, when you begin your research, your questions will probably be quite general. ("How does Wollstonecraft characterize the position of women in her society? What kinds of subjects does she cover?") To develop a good thesis, you need to take into account the questions we have been asking in this section. Below are some sample thesis statements.

FOR EXAMPLE: In the case of Essay 1, on the Apollo Program, here are two thesis statements as presented by two different authors. The first is not very effective, while the second is much more so.

THESIS

Ineffective Thesis

The Apollo Program was organized by the United States when they wanted to beat the Soviet Union to the moon. It was a race that they thought they could win, but NASA's engineers needed to solve many problems first. They made many new useful technologies while they were designing the rockets and the lunar-lander, etc. I will talk about these inventions and how they were made at NASA's laboratories during the Gemini and Apollo Programs.

This gives a topic, but it has no clear thesis statement. It intends to describe the new technologies produced during the effort to send men to the moon, but it does not tell us *why* we need to hear this. This paper will constitute a *report*, but not a research essay. University and college students must go beyond writing reports to write papers that contain an argument. In these, the author is more like a lawyer, presenting charges and supporting evidence to the jury of the author's peers—the readers. Readers want to hear you argue something *specific* about your topic. The beginning of the paper must present the thesis, and the body of the paper must present the evidence in support of that thesis.

The second thesis statement is much more effective. Note also the second author's tone, which is less casual and therefore more appropriate to a formal history paper.

> ### 👍 Better Thesis
>
> The Gemini and Apollo Programs of the 1960s and 1970s depended heavily upon new technologies and key advances in engineering. One of the technologies most critical to the success of the missions was the computer. Powerful new computers permitted the engineers and the astronauts to make important calculations very quickly, which was absolutely vital to the mission, especially in emergency situations. This paper will demonstrate that new computer technologies were one of the key advances that enabled NASA to achieve its goals of sending men to the moon.

THESIS

This second thesis statement gives the reader a concrete sense of what will be argued. The author has identified a particular theme among many potential possibilities and makes the specific argument that the role that computers played in NASA's missions was of critical importance. The reader can now expect to encounter a range of evidence in support of this clearly stated thesis. Keep in mind that, sometimes, a historical event or situation had many causes or had a range of outcomes. In those cases, it is up to the researcher to choose whether one or more of these causes is or are the most important. While there may be several (or even several thousand) reasons why a particular event took place, you will want to identify one or more of them as critical or as most important. This is one place where the metaphor of the police investigation breaks down: when you are dealing with complex historical problems, there is rarely only one right answer.

FOR EXAMPLE: In Essay 2, on Mary Wollstonecraft, we have assumed that you are not required to do any outside reading, so you may not be in a position to say a great deal about the current debates on Wollstonecraft's writing. (If your instructor has discussed such debates in lectures or has provided you with supplementary readings, these may give you a starting point.) Even so, your own reading should enable you to identify some controversial or puzzling elements in Wollstonecraft's writing. Let's return to the passage that we discussed earlier:

> Ignorance and the mistaken cunning that nature sharpens in weak heads as a principle of self-preservation, render women very fond of dress, and produce all the vanity which such fondness may naturally be expected to generate, to the exclusion of emulation and magnanimity.[10]

---

[10] Wollstonecraft, 333.

This passage suggests some useful possibilities. You might ask, for example, "What did Wollstonecraft mean by 'nature'? How does this concept function in relationship to the argument she makes in the *Vindication?*" At this point, however, you still have a topic, rather than a thesis or argument. One common error is to confuse the thesis statement—which should summarize the argument of the paper—with a restatement of the topic. In this example, a weak thesis that is actually a statement of the topic may look like this:

👎 Ineffective Thesis

In this paper, I will examine Mary Wollstonecraft's understanding of "nature" and the role this concept plays in her argument.

This statement is similar to a lawyer opening for the defence by saying, "Today, I will discuss whether my client is innocent or guilty." If you were on trial, it would be much more reassuring to hear a clear argument, such as, "My client is innocent, and all the evidence the Crown has presented is circumstantial."

Here is a much stronger thesis statement than the one above:

👍 Better Thesis

According to Mary Wollstonecraft, the natural world was governed by rational laws. As a result, both men and women were "naturally" rational creatures. On this basis, Wollstonecraft argued that women should be given the same rights as men.

This thesis statement takes a clear position and makes clear the "case" the author plans to argue in the rest of the paper.

FOR EXAMPLE: In Essay 4, on the Chinese War of Resistance, the following examples again make clear the distinction between ineffective and effective thesis statements.

👎 Ineffective Thesis

Were the Chinese Communists able to defeat the Nationalist government in 1949 because of their experience fighting the Japanese during the War of Resistance? This is an important question that can be answered by examining the words of the participants in the conflict.

In this case, the only thing that is "argued" here is that this is an important question. This statement is not a clear thesis because it makes no claim. Instead, the author has confused the idea of formulating a "research question" with the formulation of a clear argument, or claim. A clear thesis should not pose an unanswered question; it should propose an answer to that question. This author should take a stand and *decide—* did the Communists' experience versus the Japanese contribute to their victory over the Nationalist government in 1949, or not?

👍 **Better Thesis**

The Chinese War of Resistance against Japan was long and costly, but the experience earned by the Communists during the struggle benefited them greatly in their battle against the Nationalist government during the Chinese Civil War. It was this experience that enabled them to expand their area of control and ultimately to defeat the Nationalists by 1949.

This thesis is much stronger, and rather than asking an unanswered question, it makes a claim by proposing a clear *answer* to that question. Without taking a side in this debate, it is not possible to make an argument either way. In a courtroom, no prosecutor would open a trial by saying, "Over the next few hours I will discuss whether or not this person committed a crime." Instead, she or he would claim, "This person committed a crime," and would then present a clear argument in support of that claim.

3.5 PLANNING YOUR PAPER

It is crucial to set aside some time to think about the material you have collected before you begin to write your paper. This is an extension of the kind of work we discussed in section 3.3, on reading sources. If you have done your research carefully, much of your thinking will have gone on as part of your research. Now you should review your research notes, to make sure the questions you posed to yourself have been answered and to identify connections or contradictions in the material you have gathered.

Use whatever techniques help you organize your thoughts. Make lists of key words or phrases, draw diagrams that illustrate the relationships between different parts of your topic, or use a voice recorder or voice recognition software to capture your ideas as you talk them through

PLANNING

aloud. Group different topics or issues under various headings and try out different ways of clustering your ideas or arguments.

If you think you have all the connections sorted out, then stop and ask yourself whether there is anything you have overlooked. Look at the conclusions you have drawn and ask yourself, "If that is true, then what follows from it? What are the implications of that claim?" Keep pushing yourself to see if you can make your argument clearer and more sophisticated. If you are the kind of person who best develops ideas as you write, then sit down and allow yourself to write out your ideas as they come to you. Afterward, you can go back over the material and pick out the key passages, ideas, and arguments that you want to use in your essay.

The first step in planning your paper is to decide on the argument you want to make and formulate a thesis statement, which we discussed in the previous section. We have emphasized that your paper needs to make a case of some kind: it needs to *prove something*. Before you can begin writing, you have to decide what it is you want to prove. Once you have decided on the argument you intend to make and have formulated a thesis statement, you can go on to plan the rest of the essay. In a similar fashion, a prosecutor would plan his or her legal case in a logical way in an effort to convince the jury of the charges that have been made. The prosecutor must determine what evidence should be presented, which witnesses should be called to the stand, and what background information the jury will need in order to reach a verdict.

Remember that the point of the essay is to prove your thesis. What do you need to do to persuade your reader to accept the argument that you present?

FOR EXAMPLE: In the section on writing a thesis statement, we provided an example of an effective thesis statement for Essay 2. Here it is again:

> ### Thesis
>
> According to Mary Wollstonecraft, the natural world was governed by rational laws. As a result, both men and women were "naturally" rational creatures. On this basis, Wollstonecraft argued that women should be given the same rights as men.

Now, what points do you have to prove in order to make this case?

1. That Wollstonecraft believed that the natural world was governed by rational laws

PLANNING

2. That she believed that both men and women were naturally rational

3. That rational creatures deserve rights

4. That women, as rational creatures, should therefore be given rights

Each of these points could be divided easily into a number of sub-points. Under point 2, for example, you might want to make the following arguments:

a) Wollstonecraft believed that God was rational.

b) Wollstonecraft believed that men and women were created in God's image.

c) Therefore, Wollstonecraft argued that men and women were naturally rational.

You then have to find examples or evidence to support each of your claims. Imagine that each section of the essay is a file folder; you need to find material to "fill" each folder. As you go along, you may find that some folders remain quite empty, while others are overflowing. In that event, you need to rethink your plan in order to take account of the available evidence. Your reader will also find your argument easier to follow if you cluster your points into three or four major groups, especially if your essay is over 2,000 words in length. Rather than making ten or twenty separate small points, you should develop a few major points, each divided in turn into smaller sub-points. As you write the final version, however, keep in mind that many instructors discourage the use of sub-headings, preferring clear transitions from topic to topic within the text itself. (See section 3.7A for a discussion of effective transitions.) Finally, you should also keep in mind the length of the paper you have been asked to write. It is unlikely that you will be able to develop more than one or two points on each page, so remember to tailor the argument you want to make to the constraints of the assignment.

Each of your points (and, in a longer paper, your sub-points) should be developed in a separate paragraph. Each paragraph is a kind of mini-essay—it needs to make a claim (the thesis of the paragraph), to provide evidence to support that claim, and to draw out the conclusions or implications clearly. Keep this in mind while you are working on the body of your paper (see section 3.7).

Whether you make a plan in this kind of point-form structure or whether you use other diagramming techniques, remember that each step of your argument needs to advance your case. You are not simply presenting evidence on a new topic to the jury; you are taking them step-by-step toward agreement with your overall claims. Think about the way that each paragraph will prove the argument set out in your thesis statement.

NEL

PLANNING

3.6 WRITING AN INTRODUCTION

By the time you are ready to begin writing, you should already have a clear idea of the argument you want to make, the various steps that you will have to take the reader through in order to prove your case, and the kinds of evidence you will need to support your claims. A good introduction orients your reader, presents the kinds of issues or topics you intend to cover in your paper, and gives a clear sense of the argument you plan to make. Remember that the introduction is written for the benefit of the reader. It lets your reader know what to expect, and it provides clues to the reader about the direction you will take in the rest of the paper. Keep in mind that a lawyer who leaves the jury wondering whether she or he is arguing for the defence or for the prosecution is unlikely to be convincing.

One way to write an effective introduction is to move from the general to the specific, or from the familiar to the unfamiliar. Try not to be *too* general. Remember that historians are interested in questions of change over time, so opening sentences that make claims about the whole globe over several millennia are unlikely to be persuasive.

FOR EXAMPLE: Here are some examples of ineffective and effective introductory sentences for Essay 2.

Ineffective Introductory Sentence

Men have always been more powerful than women, and it seems as though this will always be the case.

Better Introductory Sentence

In the late eighteenth century, many writers believed that relationships between men and women were about to be transformed.

The second example orients the reader in time—this is a paper about the late eighteenth century. It makes a general statement that begins to focus the reader's attention on a particular historical moment. By the end of the introduction, you want the reader to have a clear sense of the argument you want to make. Recall the sample thesis statement and

INTRODUCTION

outline for this essay provided in the previous section. One possible introduction for such a paper would look like this:

> In the late eighteenth century, many writers believed that relationships between men and women were about to be transformed. After the revolution in France, there was a widespread belief that all relationships were up for debate. Writers like Mary Wollstonecraft, the English feminist, used both scientific and religious arguments to call for a revolution in relationships between the sexes. According to Wollstonecraft, the natural world was governed by rational laws. As a result, both men and women were "naturally" rational creatures. On this basis, Wollstonecraft argued that women should be given the same rights as men.

In this case, the introduction lets the reader know the topic you have chosen (Wollstonecraft's writing on nature), the historical context (the late eighteenth century, England, a time of revolution), and your argument (that Wollstonecraft appealed to nature to argue for women's rights). An effective introduction sets the tone for an effective paper, and it reassures the reader that you know what you are doing and what you want to prove.

An introduction can also be used to orient the reader, providing key dates or identifying key players.

FOR EXAMPLE: Here are some examples of ineffective and effective introductory sentences for Essay 4.

Ineffective Introductory Sentence

China is a huge country with a massive population and Mao knew that this would be his secret weapon for defeating Japan in the war and conquering all of China.

Better Introductory Sentence

During China's War of Resistance against Japan (1937–1945), the military forces of the Chinese Communists grew dramatically under the leadership of Mao Zedong (1893–1976), who had a much larger goal than simply defeating Japan.

INTRODUCTION

58

In the first example, the author's tone—using words like "huge," "massive," and "secret weapon"—is too informal for a history research paper. More importantly, this example does not present an argument. The tone of the second example is more formal, but it also suggests the author's central argument—that Mao Zedong had a larger goal. The second example also gives dates for key events and people as they are first introduced to the reader. Prosecuting a successful case requires you to provide the audience with all of the relevant information, especially in your introductory section. You need to anticipate the readers' needs, answering their questions ("which war? when was it fought?") before they even have a chance to ask them.

3.7 THE BODY OF THE PAPER: PRESENTING YOUR EVIDENCE

Now that you have formulated a clear thesis and you have an idea of what points you will make in support of that argument, you need to assemble your evidence and present it to the reader. This is the "body" of your paper. It is your opportunity to convince the reader that they should agree with your argument and that the historical evidence that you have found supports your claim. As we noted above, it is a good idea to draft a brief outline, or skeleton, of your paper before you begin. An outline allows you to be realistic about how many ideas you will be able to develop and what evidence you will need to include in support of each of those points. Build your outline logically, starting with the central argument, which you need to present in the introduction. Keep your reader in mind as you plan your essay. Which parts of your case do they need to understand first? Who are the principal actors or agents, and how are they relevant? What evidence have you found that supports your claim, and how much of it requires additional explanations or background information in order to be appreciated?

The more sophisticated and complex your argument, the more work you will have to do to assist your readers in following it. If you need to move away from your main argument to provide background information, let the reader know what you are doing. If you intend to introduce and develop a "case study," you need to let the reader know that too. Transitional phrases are not just filler—they are crucial in improving readers' experience of your paper. (See section 3.7A for more on developing effective transitions.)

BODY

A) BUILDING YOUR CASE

The body of your paper should flow logically from the initial argument you have made in the context of the introduction. As we note above, when you build your argument, you should present it in a sequence that can be easily understood by the reader. Sometimes it's important to keep things in chronological order. In the case of Essay 1, for example, the discussion of the Apollo Project's early development and its initial goals would normally precede any analysis of later launch attempts. Along the way, you need to decide how best to present the evidence you have uncovered to demonstrate that certain technical achievements were the source of the mission's success.

FOR EXAMPLE: In the case of Essay 1, you could paraphrase another author, or possibly even quote a senior administrator, as in the following paragraph:

NASA's Deputy Administrator from 1965 to 1968, Robert C. Seamans, Jr., pointed out the importance of computers to the agency's many simulated "what-if" games, and in the NASA history of the Apollo Project he writes:

> Throughout the testing, both ground and flight, we played deadly serious "what-if" games—designed to anticipate contingencies and cope successfully with them. Computers were invaluable aids to these simulation exercises. Out of these efforts came the experience and team coherence that were the backbone of Apollo's success.[1]

The Deputy Administrator's insistence upon the important role played by computers during the many rehearsals is clear. Without them, concrete measures to overcome dangerous problems such as lighting strikes and ruptured oxygen tanks could not have been prepared.

[1] Robert C. Seamans, Jr., "Foreword," in *Apollo: Expeditions to the Moon*, ed. Edgar M. Cortright (Washington: National Aeronautics and Space Administration, 1975), x.

The weight of the evidence you have collected is added to your argument to support the individual points you are making. You do not want to surprise your reader with sudden changes in your argument or to introduce evidence that contradicts your earlier claims. You need to maintain the momentum necessary for the reader to accept your conclusions.

When arguing your case, do not omit relevant details that the reader needs to understand your claims. In this case, you should probably not discuss the Apollo Project without mentioning the contemporary rocket program undertaken by the Soviet Union. The technical advances made

BODY

by German rocket scientists during the Second World War should not be neglected either, as they form the basis of later rocket programs. Related subjects such as these provide a suitable context for your central discussion. The reader may wish to know how these sorts of parallel considerations affect your analysis, and you should consider incorporating them in order to strengthen your argument and defend against possible alternative explanations. Never leave out evidence that contradicts or complicates your arguments. Find a way to incorporate that evidence into your own position, using it to develop a more complex and nuanced claim.

As your essay develops, you should connect your paragraphs together in ways that help the reader to understand where your narrative is headed next. As you move from one idea to the next, provide indicators for the reader that make it clear what you will be examining in each paragraph. You could begin a new paragraph with a phrase such as, "Of course, in addition to calculating trajectory, computers were also designed to aid the astronauts in emergency situations." This acts as a sort of road sign, helping the reader to make the transition from one idea to the next.

FOR EXAMPLE: In the case of Essay 4, here is one way to make a transition from discussing the recruiting of Chinese guerrilla fighters to the importance of training young officers. After dealing with the first issue, you need to draw out your conclusions and provide a connection to the next theme.

BODY

👍👍 **Effective Transition**

In this way, the Communists were able to move behind Japanese lines and recruit thousands of Chinese peasants who were willing to fight.

The process of recruitment, however, involved more than just finding able-bodied villagers. These locals needed to be educated about the Communists' revolutionary agenda, and here the Communists relied upon young officer cadres who could both fight and teach.

Here the author has made an effective transition between two distinct themes. This reassures your readers by letting them know what the "pay-off" of the next paragraph is going to be. It helps readers to follow your narrative as you move from one part of your essay to another, and prepares them to hear about new themes and new evidence in support of your claim.

B) QUOTING AND PARAPHRASING YOUR SOURCES

Throughout this guide, we emphasize the need to make a case in your paper. Making a case requires more than just good writing or a forceful statement of your position. You also need to support your arguments with evidence and examples and to demonstrate (and not merely assert) your claims. Primary sources—such as contemporary articles, diaries, and speeches—are usually the best evidence. If you are quoting secondary sources, remember that they should be used only to support and not to replace your own arguments. Quoting a secondary source at length is like using another author's words to write your essay for you. It is also acceptable to reproduce brief quotations from primary sources that you have found in secondary sources. (See the example on p. 48.) If you are pointing out a disagreement between two authors, or a difference between your claims and those of a published work, it would be appropriate to quote directly from the secondary source. (See the example on p. 44.) Also, remember that quotations do not "speak for themselves." What seems obvious about a passage to you may not be obvious at all to your reader, so it is important to introduce your quote appropriately in order to help the reader understand its relevance.

When should I quote a source directly? You should incorporate quotations from primary sources only when they support your argument directly and are necessary to make your case. Try to avoid unnecessarily long quotations, as they break up your argument. (Hurried readers may even skip over them so keep them short and to the point.) A long passage, reprinted without commentary from you, will not help make your case. It may even confuse the reader, who may draw a range of conclusions, perhaps quite different from those you intend, from the material. Using long quotations simply to fill space is not effective writing. If you do use a long quoted passage, you need to go back to emphasize and comment on the elements you see as key to your argument. Here is an example of a quotation from a historical subject from Essay 4:

> Chinese Communist leader Mao Zedong believed that a Chinese victory over Japan in the War of Resistance would require the mobilization of large numbers of Chinese citizens. Even before the war began, he said in a 1936 interview that, "Besides employing trained armies to carry on mobile warfare, we must organize great numbers of guerrilla units among the peasants."[1]

[1] Mao Zedong, interview with Edgar Snow, 16 July 1936, quoted in "On Protracted War," *Selected Works of Mao Zedong*, Vol. II (Peking: Foreign Languages Press, 1967), 120.

Here, the author of the essay has made a claim about Mao's *beliefs*, and making claims about how a person felt or what they believed generally requires direct evidence. Therefore, the author has provided a quotation that demonstrates Mao Zedong's beliefs very directly, giving the reader more confidence in the author's claim.

At each point, the evidence presented should be relevant and placed in context. Always remember to identify your speakers. Quotations should be introduced by naming the speaker and by providing the reader with the information necessary to appreciate the significance of the evidence presented. When was the statement made? In what context? The material quoted should have a clear and obvious relationship to the claim you use to introduce it. You should also make sure that the words and phrases you use to introduce the quotation make sense with the quoted material; if necessary, rephrase your introductory statements so that the quoted material fits smoothly.

👍👍 Appropriate Use of a Quotation

For Mary Wollstonecraft, God was reasonable: "Rational religion [...] is a submission to the will of a being so perfectly wise, that all he wills must be directed by the proper motive—must be reasonable."[1]

[1] Wollstonecraft, 329.

This quotation demonstrates the claim that Wollstonecraft believed that God was rational by quoting a passage in which she states that a being who was "perfectly wise" would always act reasonably. Note that we have deleted a short phrase in this passage ("on the contrary"), which is here represented by ellipses or a series of three dots enclosed in square brackets ([...]). Because this phrase refers to an earlier sentence in Wollstonecraft's work that we have not quoted, it would be pointless to include it. Be careful, however, not to omit words or phrases that would change the meaning of a passage. Also make sure that you do not take phrases out of context. It would be inappropriate, for example, to use this passage in the following way:

👎 Inappropriate Use of a Quotation

Mary Wollstonecraft believed that all religion was oppressive, because it involved "submission to the will of a being" outside ourselves.[1]

[1] Wollstonecraft, 329.

By providing quotations, you are attempting to prove to your reader that the point you make is a valid one. Be aware, however, that misrepresenting your source material is like planting false evidence in a police investigation. It is never acceptable. The second quotation is used in an attempt to support a blanket statement about Wollstonecraft's beliefs for which no clear evidence is provided.

Can I quote another author's words as found in a secondary source? While quoting secondary sources is less common, as we discussed above, it can be a useful way of comparing the arguments or ideas of two or more authors, both of whom are authorities on a given topic.

FOR EXAMPLE: Here is an example from Essay 3, in which the author is analyzing a passage from Paul DePasquale's article on encounters between Europeans and First Nations peoples. DePasquale is contrasting his own views with those of the writer Umberto Eco, and he quotes Eco in the process:

> Paul DePasquale, for example, emphasizes the differences between his approach and that taken by the Italian theorist Umberto Eco:
>
> > My reading complicates the assumption that the process of writing about the new world was a straightforward one that involved little more than the transportation to foreign places of existing classical, biblical, and medieval images, or what Umberto Eco calls "background books." Eco emphasizes the role of this baggage:
> >
> > > [W]e travel with preconceived notions of the world, derived from our cultural tradition. In a very curious sense we travel knowing in advance what we are on the verge of discovering, because past reading has told us what we are supposed to discover.[8]
> >
> > DePasquale does not reject the idea that the Europeans carried "baggage" when they came to the new world, but he places more emphasis than Eco does on the role of Aboriginal peoples in challenging Europeans' "preconceived notions of the world."

[8] Umberto Eco, *Serendipities: Language and Lunacy,* trans. William Weaver (New York: Columbia University Press, 1998), 54–55. Quoted in DePasquale, "Worth the Noting," 9.

In this case, your footnote should include the citation for both sources—the author you are quoting and the author he or she is quoting. (See Chapter 4 for details.)

64

Note: Because the quoted passage is quite long, it has been set off as a *block quotation*. Block quotations should be indented on the left side, and they do not require quotation marks. They are offset paragraphs, but while they appear to stand on their own, remember to set them up appropriately, so that the reader knows whom you are quoting.

You can also use quotations from secondary sources to provide not only the author's argument but also his or her evidence, as in the following example, also from Essay 3.

> Some seventeenth-century commentators justified their desire to exploit the wealth of the colonies as a way of fulfilling God's plan for the conversion of Native peoples. According to Paul DePasquale, "Writing in 1609, for example, Virginia Company of London promoter Robert Johnson constructed English greed as an integral part of God's plan to propagate the gospel among Indians: '[S]ome object wee seeke nothing lesse than the cause of God, beeing led on by our owne private ends,' he wrote."[9]

[9] Robert Johnson, *Nova Britannia* (London: S. Macham, 1609; repr., in D. B. Quinn, ed., *New American World: A Documentary History of North America to 1612,* New York: Arno Press, 1979), 5: 239. As cited in DePasquale, "Worth the Noting," 11.

Note: DePasquale reproduces Johnson's words exactly. Sometimes authors insert the term "sic" (which is Latin for "so" or "thus") to call attention to the fact that there was an error in the original text. In this case, DePasquale assumes that the reader will recognize that the entire passage is rendered in an archaic spelling.

What is paraphrasing? Paraphrasing is the rephrasing of someone else's statements or writings in order to convey their ideas in your own words. This technique is often used when discussing a secondary source, such as a biography, monograph, or textbook. If you want to relate the substance of an author's idea or ideas without copying out their text verbatim (exactly as it appears), you must reformulate the passage, expressing it in your own words, and then cite the source just as you would if you were quoting directly. Remember that when you are paraphrasing, you are still making use of someone else's work, so even though it is not an exact duplication of a passage, it must still be cited.

FOR EXAMPLE: The following passages are taken from Essay 4. The first entry is a direct quotation from the book *Thunder out of China*, by co-authors Theodore H. White and Annalee Jacoby, while the second paraphrases their words.

BODY

Sample Quotation

In reflecting upon the struggle of the Chinese Communists against the Japanese during China's War of Resistance, Theodore White and Annalee Jacoby wrote, "Most of the Communist expansion was directed against the Japanese, but they fought government troops when necessary too, and as they reported attacks on themselves in broad new areas of penetration behind the Japanese lines, they sounded like the man who claimed he had been hit in the fist with the other fellow's eye."[11]

Although occasional brief quotations from secondary sources can support your claims, it is not advisable to quote such long phrases, so you should put it into your own words:

Paraphrased Version

In addition to fighting against the Japanese during the War of Resistance, Communist troops sometimes fought with Chinese government forces, and it was not always clear which side had attacked the other.[11]

The paraphrased example includes the same material and the same ideas, but it has been rewritten in the essay writer's own words, which allows the material to be expressed more concisely and to be better incorporated into the text. Paraphrasing can also be a very useful way to include the ideas or claims of those commenting on or participating in an event without including long quotations. Whether you are quoting directly or paraphrasing, remember to include a footnote or an endnote to acknowledge your source.

C) KEEPING THE READER IN MIND: DEFINING YOUR TERMS CLEARLY

As we noted above, it is critical to keep the reader in mind as you are planning and writing your essay. If the reader has to work hard to make connections or to figure out the context for your arguments, they will be less likely to be carried along by the force of your argument. If, for example, your thesis involved arguing that there were particular technological advances in rocket science that made the Apollo lunar project possible, you would need to make this subject and time frame understood to the reader in the introduction. As the paper went on, you

---

[11] Theodore H. White and Annalee Jacoby, *Thunder out of China* (New York: William Sloane Associates, 1946), 211.

BODY

would need to identify the principal agents and actors involved in the project, such as NASA and astronaut Neil Armstrong. Key terms, such as "NASA" and "escape velocity," would require definitions, which should appear conveniently in the text as each term is introduced.

Defining key terms helps the reader understand your case. In a courtroom, expert witnesses could be called upon by the prosecutor to explain difficult concepts to the jury. The jury may well be composed of intelligent people, but they are unlikely to be familiar with all of the technical details of the case. Likewise, in an essay, you must provide definitions, to avoid having the reader ask, "What does that term mean?" Of course, obvious terms, such as "earth" and "moon," require no explanation. The task of distinguishing between terms that require definitions and those that do not is up to the author. Experience over time in presenting your work in a written format will make this distinction easier. If you are uncertain, consult your instructor.

3.8 WRITING FOR YOUR AUDIENCE: TIPS TO CONSIDER AND PITFALLS TO AVOID

Do not write with any particular instructor in mind. Write for a broader audience such as your classmates. If there is a new topic or term that you learned while investigating your case, define it for your audience as well. If there is a particularly complex technical point, try to summarize it briefly before proceeding with your argument. Your reader may already know the term you have defined, but there is no harm in defining it anyway. Clear definitions make your argument easier to appreciate.

It is also important to think carefully about your word choices. Avoid unnecessarily complex language when writing your essay. Literary gymnastics are not essential elements of a well-written, coherent, convincing paper. The overuse of big words—especially if they are not used correctly—could be off-putting for your audience. You should never rely on "academic-sounding" words to sound authoritative and convincing. You should also pay attention to the words you use to introduce your points and quotations. As we noted in our discussion of reading secondary sources, words like "argues," "recognizes," or "identifies" all have slightly different meanings. "Argues" emphasizes the contribution the author is making to a debate, while "identifies" or "recognizes" suggests (rightly or wrongly) that the point is a commonly accepted or uncontroversial one. The way that you phrase your claims helps to shape the way your readers interpret them.

TIPS/PITFALLS

Remember, your argument is based on the assembly and analysis of the works and arguments of others, and you are not expected to be an absolute authority on the subject. The key aspect of the exercise is to learn to deal critically with diverse sources as evidence to further a particular argument. Your instructor will not expect you to have become an expert in the field over the course of a few short weeks, but she or he will expect you to write with confidence and assurance. Take your time and learn to have faith in your ability to think critically and write effectively.

When researching and writing your essay, consider these tips:

- *Consult several sources when researching your paper.* If you rely simply on one or two sources, or primarily on very old sources, your argument could appear unbalanced or out of date.

- *Write history in the past tense.* Events of long ago, or even of yesterday, belong to the past and should be referred to in that tense. Certain types of sources, however, such as novels and philosophical works, are often written about in a kind of "eternal present"; the present tense should be used when dealing with them.

- *Choose simple words.* Overwhelming your audience with big words can be counterproductive. For example, "The television commentator was quite sesquipedalian," can be expressed more simply as "The television commentator enjoyed using big words." Forcing your audience to look up definitions for your terms will not enhance your argument. Be especially careful when using a thesaurus; make sure you understand and know how to use the words you find there. A thesaurus might offer "Handmaidens had no bi-partisan powers in this epoch" as a replacement for "Women had few political rights in this period," but the two sentences are clearly not equivalent; in fact, the more straightforward version is much more effective.

- *Provide dates when introducing historical events or people:*
the Great Kanto Earthquake of 1 September 1923

- *Capitalize historic events and adjectives derived from proper nouns:*
Sino-Japanese War, Communist ideology, the Western world

- *Capitalize official titles when providing names (but not on their own):*
He met Prime Minister Trudeau on 1 June 1971.
     He met the prime minister on 1 June 1971.
They informed Emperor Hirohito.
     They informed the emperor.

> U.S. Attorney General Janet Reno went to Washington.
> The U.S. attorney general went to Washington.

- *Capitalize religious, national, or ethnic names:*
  Indigenous peoples, Soviet satellite, Protestantism
- *Always italicize foreign words:*
  The queen ate *sukiyaki* for the first time.
  Hitler ordered the *Luftwaffe* to bomb London.
  Samurai were expected to follow the code of *bushido.*

Here are some common pitfalls you should avoid:

- *Avoid long, wordy sentences.* Keep your statements direct and to the point, not weighed down with unnecessary or repetitious commentary. Redundant phrasing, such as "eventual subsequent consequences" and "the need for this essential necessity," sounds awkward. You may be tempted to try to sound authoritative, like the narrator of a documentary film, but overly dramatic language will undermine the effectiveness of your argument. Keep it simple, and your audience will have an easier time grasping your point.
- *Avoid sweeping generalizations.* Your argument will sound less convincing if you resort to broad or obvious assertions, such as, "Wars have been fought by tribes and nations since the dawn of mankind" or "Throughout history, humanity has been faced by countless natural disasters." Such generalizations are particularly irritating to historians because the emphasis of the discipline is on change over time.
- *Do not let the dictionary define your terms.* Avoid beginning your essay with a quotation or a dictionary definition, such as "The Gage Canadian Dictionary defines 'communism' as ...." This is a clichéd way to begin a paper. In any case, dictionary definitions are frequently irrelevant because the sense of a word may have changed dramatically over time. In fact, the way in which a word or concept has changed might even be the chief point of a research paper. If you have been asked to write about the way an author in the past uses a word or concept, then signal your intention to focus on the changing meanings of the word by setting it off in quotation marks the first time you use it: "Mary Wollstonecraft's understanding of 'virtue' was closely linked to what she called 'nature.'"
- *Avoid using contractions (even though we've occasionally used them in this guide!).* Spell out phrases such as "do not," "should not," "cannot" and "will not." Contractions such as "don't,"

"shouldn't," "can't" and "won't" are not appropriate in formal writing assignments.

- *Do not editorialize.* Keep your argument focused on the sources and incorporate them to support your case. Although your topic may be dramatic or controversial, avoid including your own personal opinion. Statements such as "the government's decision was idiotic" or "hers was the greatest victory ever" reflect the author's own opinion—but that is not the object of an essay. The reader wants to be convinced of the merits of your case based on the evidence you have collected; he or she does not want to hear your personal opinion on the subject.

- *Avoid making casual self-references.* Be careful about identifying yourself casually within the text of your paper with the terms "I," "me," or "my." Some instructors prefer that you refer to "this paper" or sometimes to "this author" if you need to refer directly to your own argument, as in, "This paper argues that ...." or "In an interview with the author, Mrs. Jones said ...." Above all, remember that the entire paper is *your argument.* Your instructor assumes that these are your claims, and it is not necessary to continually draw attention to that fact. While some instructors may be sympathetic to the occasional use of "I argue," references to "I feel" or "I wish" that cannot be supported by evidence are not appropriate in a history essay.

- *Avoid using the passive voice.* The use of the passive voice in writing is usually associated with a weak argument that cannot name or identify its agents. If the reader needs to ask, "To whom are you referring here?" then you are probably using the passive voice. An *active* construction would read, "The government took several steps to address the problem," while a *passive* construction would read, "Several steps were taken to address the problem." In the second construction, what happened to the government? It is not clear what agent or actor undertook the action. Similarly, "several expeditions were launched" or "a new project was undertaken" both employ the passive voice. Be explicit when making statements such as these. You should not leave the audience to guess at or to assume the identity of the agent performing the action. The passive voice can sometimes be useful (for example, when you want to emphasize the action rather than the actors) but it should be used sparingly.

- *Avoid using colloquial language and slang phrases.* Colloquial language is not appropriate in a research paper or an essay, and you should avoid it. Phrases such as "airy-fairy" and "hothead

70

countries" are not clear or objective. Choose your words carefully, for they can be very powerful tools. Also, some phrases used in everyday speech do not sound as effective on paper. For example, "He got picked by the army" would sound better as, "He was selected by the army" or "He was chosen by the army." Similarly, "They just didn't get it" should be rephrased as, "They did not understand." Use your judgment—and remember that writing in your own words is best.

- *Avoid using mixed metaphors.* Be careful not to mix metaphors when describing something. To say that "the army tore down the fortress walls like a tornado and flooded in through the gates" is a mixed metaphor because the concepts of tornado and flood do not match.

- *Mobilize the evidence, not emotion, in support of your case.* Do not try to persuade the reader by appealing to their emotions. Your argument should rely on evidence rather than attempting to manipulate your reader into accepting your claims.

3.9 DRAWING CONCLUSIONS: MAKING EFFECTIVE CLOSING ARGUMENTS

Finally, your paper should draw strong conclusions. These conclusions should reflect the argument you stated in the introduction and summarize the material you have presented for the final consideration of the reader. In a courtroom, this phase consists of the prosecutor's closing arguments, designed to encapsulate the case and persuade the jury to accept the conclusions drawn from the evidence. Restating your case brings the reader back to your initial claims, which can now be considered in the light of the evidence you have presented.

FOR EXAMPLE: The following examples illustrate effective and ineffective conclusions to Essay 4.

Ineffective Conclusion

That is why the Chinese Communists won the civil war against the Nationalists in 1949. If they hadn't fought so hard to beat Japan, they never would have learned how to fight like guerrillas. Then the Communists probably would have lost the civil war.

CONCLUSIONS

This conclusion states the writer's opinion very clearly, but it does not review the paper's argument or its evidence adequately. It also poses an alternative outcome that never took place and the likelihood of which can never be proven. Rather than resorting to emotional appeals or generalizations, a solid conclusion must refresh the reader's memory and bring the paper back to the beginning—to what was being argued at the outset. Then, it must review briefly the evidence that has been presented.

👍 Better Conclusion

As this paper has argued, the 1949 victory of the Communists in the Chinese Civil War was fuelled by the experience the Communists earned while fighting against the Japanese during the War of Resistance. The Communist effort to recruit peasants, especially those behind Japanese lines, was key to their struggle against Japan. The peasants' importance has been made clear through the words of the cadres who educated them about the Communists' revolutionary agenda. After Japan's surrender in 1945, the Communists were then able to conquer the whole of China by incorporating peasant guerrilla fighters into their People's Liberation Army. Their victory over China's Nationalist government in 1949 was an extension of Mao Zedong's plan for Protracted War, which, as we have seen, he first proposed in a series of lectures in May 1938.

This conclusion is much stronger, and it restates the author's argument very clearly. It also reviews the evidence that has been discussed within the body of the paper, in much the same way that a prosecutor would remind the jury during closing arguments of the importance of the testimony and the evidence that has been presented. Ending a paper abruptly leaves the reader hanging, losing an important opportunity to refresh the reader's memory and highlight the key material that you have introduced in support of your case.

Avoid ending a paper by posing a question. To conclude with a rhetorical question such as, "Will humanity ever learn that war is never the answer?" is an empty line of inquiry that will usually cause readers to roll their eyes rather than inspire reflection. Keep your conclusion focused on the evidence that supports your argument and summarize your position concisely. If your paper opens up new lines of inquiry that have yet to be examined by scholars, mentioning them is an effective way to conclude your paper. Here are some further examples of effective conclusions from Essays 2 and 3.

CONCLUSIONS

👍 Effective Conclusion

Wollstonecraft's justification for women's emancipation thus draws on both science and religion, complicating our understanding of the Enlightenment as a time when religion was replaced by science. Wollstonecraft used science to try to demonstrate that rationality was the "natural" state for human beings. In her comments on religion, she also argued that God was "naturally" rational. Since she believed that men and women were created in God's image, then as long as they were not forced to act against their own natures by society, both men and women were rational beings. Since society had forced women to act unnaturally, they had (naturally) become irrational. Wollstonecraft's goal was to allow women the freedom to be both natural and reasonable.

👍 Effective Conclusion

Brown and Vibert are correct in asserting that many postcolonial scholars have come to assume that "in representing their encounters with indigenous peoples, Euro-Americans were writing about themselves as much as they were writing about others." As we have seen, however, there are still many scholars working in the field who reject the assumption that the "postcolonial" is a relevant category in Canada, where colonialism continues to exert an important influence on the lives of First Nations people. Furthermore, any understanding of the encounter between Euro-Americans and First Nations peoples must recognize the agency of both groups. This is especially important because the question of Aboriginal agency continues to play a key role in political debates over issues such as land claims and residential schools.

CONCLUSIONS

In both cases, the conclusion reviews the major elements of the argument that the paper has developed and points to the larger implications of the claims. In the second example, the concluding line suggests how the kind of scholarship that has been discussed remains relevant to contemporary political debates. Note, however, that neither example goes beyond the scope of the paper to make general claims about the nature of relationships between the sexes or the futility of political change. Pay attention to the way in which the articles and books you read for your class draw their conclusions and try to model your own conclusions on those examples.

3.10 FORMATTING AND EDITING RESEARCH ESSAYS IN HISTORY

You should be careful to follow precisely any instructions you have been given about formatting and layout. Generally, the formatting tips below are appropriate in history papers, which often follow particular written conventions.

A) WORKING WITH DATES

Dates in good historical writing usually appear *without commas*:

- Jimmy Jones visited London on 21 April 2001.
- On 4 June of that year, he met Queen Elizabeth II (1926–).
- Then, on 17 June, the queen sent him a letter.
- He replied on 22 June.
- Between 3 and 8 July he travelled to Scotland.

Always provide dates when introducing major events and important historical persons for the first time:

- Between the First World War (1914–1918) and the Second World War (1939–1945), there were many smaller conflicts.
- Japanese Prime Minister Katō Takaaki (1860–1926) was educated in Tokyo.
- Former U.S. President Bill Clinton (1946–) visited Spain in 2001.

When discussing a decade or a century, no apostrophe is needed:

- The 1960s and 1970s were very turbulent.
- The 1700s and 1800s were times of rapid change.

B) WORKING WITH NUMBERS

Use *words* for numbers between one and nine:

- The plan called for six agents, but only five were hired.

Use *Arabic numerals* for numbers 10 and over, except for millions/billions:

- The 12 new submarines cost US$75 million each.

Always use words to describe centuries:

- The nineteenth century was a time of imperial expansion; the twentieth has been a period of decolonization.

If you must begin a sentence with a number, use words:

- Fifteen people fell into the water, but only 11 were rescued.

Use Arabic numerals for numbers with decimal places:

- 8.5, 12.3 billion

Write fractions out in words:

- one-third, two-thirds, three-fifths

Use appropriate symbols for world currencies in the following way:

- The program cost the government US$400 billion.
- The robbers got away with AU$300 million.
- The Sony Corporation reported a profit of ¥500 million.
- Nigel won £67,000, but lost it all at the casino.
- The plan is expected to cost €4.75 million.

C) WORKING WITH NAMES

Always use *full names and dates* when introducing historical persons for the first time, and subsequently use last names only:

> Mary Wollstonecraft (1759–1797) is often considered an early feminist. At the same time, Wollstonecraft's views on women are very different from those held by most contemporary feminists.

D) EDITING CHECKLIST

Finally, here is an editing checklist to help you format your paper. It is a good idea to follow it while you write, in order to minimize the amount of editing required later, but you can always review it when you finish writing. Every author has their own approach to editing. With practice, you will be able to format your paper correctly as you write. If your instructor has specific suggestions, be sure to follow them.

- Have you started your text at the very top of page one?
- Have all unnecessary spaces in the text been deleted?
- Is your text double-spaced, and in a 12-point font?
- Is the paper in the past tense?
- Is the introduction concise, and does it state your claim/thesis clearly?
- Are historical persons and events introduced in full with dates?

FORMATTING/EDITING

- Are all numbers and dates formatted correctly and consistently?
- Are book titles, periodical titles, and foreign words *italicized*?
- Are terms like "the Western world" capitalized consistently?
- Are all of your pages numbered, including the bibliography?
- Does the paper flow logically and demonstrate its case?
- Does the evidence presented support your claim?
- Have you summarized your argument and your findings in the conclusion?
- Are block quotations offset from your text and indented on both sides?
- Have all speakers or authors been identified before quoting them?
- Have all the necessary facts or paraphrased ideas been referenced/cited?
- Do reference/citation numbers appear correctly as "... quotation."[27]?
- Are footnotes/endnotes formatted correctly? (See Chapter 4.)
- Did you include a separate bibliography and list all the sources that you have cited, alphabetically, by author's last name?
- Have you filled out the required title page in full?

Choose a title for your paper *after* it is complete. The title is the very first thing that your reader will see; for that reason, it should make your topic and its importance very clear. A title such as "Assignment 1" provides no indication of your topic or argument. Wait until your paper is finished and you know precisely what it is arguing. Do not leave the reader to guess what your title means or how it is relevant to the essay or the course. Your title sets the tone for your paper. Be aware of your audience as you develop it.

FOR EXAMPLE: In the case of Essay 1, on the Apollo Program, the subject being discussed in the essay is the critical importance of computer technology in the "space race." The essay argues that it was recent advances in computer capability that enabled NASA to send men to the moon. Consider the appropriateness of these titles:

Ineffective Title

The Apollo Missions to the Moon
Reader's response: "What about them?"

Ineffective Title

"Blast Off!" NASA's Quest to Put a Man on the Moon
Reader's response: "When is the DVD coming out?"

Better Title

How Improvements in Computers Helped NASA to Land Men on the Moon in 1969
Reader's response: "Okay, that's pretty straightforward."

Effective Title

Supercomputers and the U.S. Apollo Missions
Reader's response: "I see. Tell me more."

Finally, create a detailed *title page* that includes all of the following:

- The title you have chosen for your essay
- Your name and student number
- The course, section, and tutorial number: History 125 (002) L2D
- The name of your professor or teaching assistant
- The name of your institution
- The date your assignment was submitted

3.11 PROOFREADING YOUR PAPER

This final and important phase is your opportunity to go back over the paper to make sure that all of the points we raised in section 3.5, on planning, and section 3.10, on formatting and editing, have been covered. Ideally, you should set the paper aside for a few days. When you come

PROOFREADING

back to it again, you may see gaps in the argument that were not visible when you were immersed in the writing process. With a fresh perspective you will also be able to see where your text requires further editing and ideas that require further clarification.

As you prepare to submit your paper, do the following:

- *Make sure that you have a clear thesis and that you support your argument effectively.* Is there a clear thesis statement near the beginning of your essay? Does each paragraph advance that thesis in a clear and obvious way? Do you provide sufficient evidence to persuade the reader to accept each of your claims? Are the connections within and among paragraphs obvious? Does each paragraph end by drawing clear conclusions that inform the reader of the implications you want them to draw? If you tend to think as you write, you will probably find that you need to do a substantial amount of editing at this point. You may also find it helpful to go back over the paper to create a "reverse outline." Create an outline version, summarizing the main argument of each paragraph in a few words. Instead of laying out a plan for what you intend to argue in the paper, you are giving yourself an opportunity to see what you have actually accomplished. Does each point follow logically from the one that precedes it? Have you allowed yourself to get distracted and introduce digressions or irrelevant material? Have you done everything you said you would do? If necessary, go back and rewrite the introduction or the thesis statement to reflect any changes that were introduced in the course of writing.

- *Double-check all of your sources and quotations.* Have you cited your sources accurately? Have you given the right page number and supplied all of the relevant publication information? Have you copied all direct quotations accurately?

- *Read your work aloud.* Reading the paper to yourself may feel awkward at first, but it is a very effective method of initial proofreading that any writer can use to identify problems in his or her text. After staring at your paper for several hours, you may miss obvious errors in grammar, spelling, or terminology. Take a break, then come back to your writing at a later time and read it aloud—slowly.

- *Have someone proofread your work.* Some students are too shy or embarrassed to let others read their work—you should not let that get in your way! Approach someone you trust who you feel writes and speaks well. Ask this person to read your paper with

PROOFREADING

a pencil in hand. Be proud of your work and have confidence in your ability to improve your writing with practice and time. Most people are flattered to be asked and will undoubtedly be interested in what you have written. Working at writing well should not be a solo endeavour—all professional historians depend on colleagues and editors to improve their work before it is published. At the same time, you should not depend too much on the help of others. One word of warning: the work you submit should represent your own efforts, not those of an "editor" who has effectively written the paper for you. Employing someone to write a paper for you is a form of academic dishonesty and is never acceptable. Keep a copy of notes and earlier drafts so that you are able to demonstrate which elements of the paper are your own work.

- *Reread your paper with a critical eye.* Efficient writing requires a minimum of effort to read, and grammar, spelling, and punctuation are all important in conveying your ideas effectively. Refer to section 3.8 and make sure you have followed the advice given there.

3.12 WHEN YOU GET YOUR PAPER BACK

No matter how much work you put into your paper at this point, it will probably be returned to you with comments and questions or with suggestions on how it might be improved. This chart summarizes the major points we have made in this chapter, and gives you some idea of the things that instructors are likely to be thinking about as they mark your paper.

In some courses, you may be asked to submit different drafts of your work over time, in which case you have an opportunity to rework the paper and submit a new version. This process is actually very similar to the process that professional historians go through when submitting a book or article manuscript for consideration at a journal or an academic press. In most cases, the manuscript is sent out to expert readers for review, and even successful papers are returned to the author with requests for changes and improvements. Take your instructor's comments as an opportunity to improve your skills as a historical researcher and writer. Ideally, the comments you receive can be part of an ongoing conversation in which you and your instructor work together to find ways to enhance and improve your research and writing skills.

Guide to Common Essay Grading Criteria

	Argument and Organization	Content/Research	Style
Excellent	A clear, original, persuasive, and sophisticated argument with a provocative thesis that takes on a clearly defined set of debates in the field.	Makes excellent use of evidence and background material; interprets and uses evidence with sensitivity to the nature of the text(s) and of historical contexts.	Well-written, elegant and clear with appropriate documentation and other scholarly apparatus.
Very Good	Well-organized, with a clear and coherent thesis statement and argument, demonstrating real understanding of the historical issues at stake; may need to be encouraged to ask more difficult questions.	Very good use of evidence (where relevant, from a range of sources), with clear understanding of the nature of the evidence and its historical context.	Well-written on the whole, though there may be some passages that are unclear or require further explication; good use of citations, etc.
Good	A clear thesis and argument, though not necessarily a particularly original or creative one; some attempt to synthesize or draw conclusions.	Good use of evidence, clear understanding of the basic elements of the texts under discussion and their uses; meets minimum in terms of research done; no major problems of interpretation.	Some problems of spelling, grammar, word choice or style, though not sufficient to entirely obscure the points being made; basic scholarly apparatus intact.
Fair	Some effort to develop a basic argument, though it may be unevenly or inadequately developed; banal approach/ question (or one that simply restates discussions we have had in class).	Some use of evidence; only just meets basic minimum in terms of research done; some problems of understanding or interpretation.	Confusing or vague, requiring a real effort on the part of the reader to guess at the arguments being made or their implications; problems with spelling, grammar, word choice and style.
Poor	No clear thesis or argument/purely descriptive; argument is ahistorical and polemical with no real attention to questions posed in the assignment.	Fails to use evidence from the text adequately or competently; inappropriate or misunderstood examples; significant problems of understanding or interpretation.	Poorly written, significant problems with grammar and word choice, difficult to understand or follow basic claims; failure to properly identify or cite passages quoted.

Citations: Documenting Your Claims

Maquinna, leader of the Mowachaht in the late eighteenth century, at the time of Captain Cook's landing on the west coast of Vancouver Island.
Oregon Historical Society, #105047

INTRODUCTION

Citing and checking references can be boring, but citations are critical to historical writing. Proper citations are essential for two reasons: they allow other researchers to identify and evaluate the sources of your claims, and they allow you to acknowledge the places where you have drawn on other people's work. Remember that submitting someone else's words or ideas without acknowledging the original author is a serious academic offence. We will discuss plagiarism and academic dishonesty in more detail below, in section 4.2, but here we want to emphasize that plagiarism is very easily avoided by making careful research notes and citing your sources carefully when quoting or paraphrasing the work of others.

When drafting your citations, remember two key things: keep the format of the citations consistent and take your time. A bibliography of works cited takes time to assemble, so putting it together at 2 a.m. the night before the paper is due is not recommended. The choice of whether to use footnotes or endnotes is often up to you, but in either case a bibliography or works cited list is also necessary.

4.1 COMMON QUESTIONS ABOUT CITATIONS: WHEN AND WHY TO USE THEM

Here are some frequently asked questions about citing sources and including quotations in your papers. The examples given here are based on the Fifteenth Edition of *The Chicago Manual of Style*. If you have further questions, speak with your instructor.

Is there a difference between citations and references? No. These two terms mean the same thing—giving the information that identifies (or "cites") your source for a quote, idea, or figure. This citation then "refers" the reader to your source, making it clear where you found that item (your "reference").

What kinds of things do I need to cite? You need to cite all direct quotations, as well as the sorts of facts and ideas that lie outside what is generally considered to be common knowledge. Obscure or little-known facts should be cited to help the reader understand what you mean and where you found such information. For example, it is commonly known that the atomic bombing of Hiroshima occurred on 6 August 1945—this fact does not require citation or an explanatory footnote. The fact that the bomb released energy equivalent to approximately 15,000 tons of TNT, however, is a sufficiently obscure fact to require citation. You should therefore provide a footnote or an endnote to allow the reader to follow up on your claim, supporting your argument with a citation. A number in superscript (on the upper part of a line) is then used to direct the reader's attention to a corresponding footnote or endnote. This number would look like this: [1]. (Note that the proper punctuation order is normally as follows: final word, period, quotation marks, and *then* the reference number. When using a colon or semi-colon, the punctuation comes after the quotation marks. The reference number always appears *last*.) There are no hard-and-fast rules to determine what sorts of things require citation—experience and practice will make this distinction easier. You should, however, always provide citations in the following cases:

- When you make a direct quotation of someone else's words.
- When you quote, summarize, or paraphrase important ideas or controversial arguments from other scholars.

CITATION

- When you use any little-known facts or figures, such as the distance between the earth and the sun (8.31 minutes at the speed of light) or the mass of the Saturn V rocket (3,038,500 kilograms). Whether information is commonly known or not depends in part on context—knowledge that is common among astrophysicists (or in some historical fields) may not be well known in others. You will need to use your best judgment in these cases.

Endnotes or footnotes can also be used to provide the following information:

- Translations for words or phrases in foreign languages that the reader could not be expected to understand and that are not commonly used in English-language sources.
- Additional information or explanation of technical points, if such information might aid the reader.

What if I am including several facts or ideas in a single paragraph? Do I have to include a footnote after every sentence? No, if you include several facts or ideas within a single paragraph, they are more conveniently cited at the end of the paragraph in a single footnote or endnote. This method eliminates the need to include a footnote at the end of every sentence, which can be tedious for both the author and the reader. You should never use lots of citations just to appear authoritative. Keep your citations focused on the evidence you present and the facts or ideas you convey to the reader.

When should I quote a source directly? You should incorporate quotations from primary sources only when they support your argument directly and are crucial to the demonstration of your case. Do not employ unnecessarily long quotations—they can distract the reader and break up your argument. Keep them short and to the point.

How do I insert those little reference numbers in my text? Most word processing programs have an "insert" function that allows you to choose either footnotes or endnotes. Make sure you choose Arabic numerals (1, 2, 3) rather than Roman numerals (i, ii, iii). Each time you insert a footnote, it will appear automatically at the foot of each page, while endnotes automatically appear at the very end of your paper. The insert-reference function is very useful because whenever you add or delete a footnote, the program will renumber all of the other notes accordingly. (Years ago, this had to be done by hand!) Whether you use footnotes or endnotes, you must still provide an alphabetized bibliography or works cited list.

CITATION

Because it is so easy to add, delete, or reorder footnotes and endnotes in most word processing programs it is very easy to make errors when using *ibid.* (in the same place) or *op. cit.* (in the work quoted) as they must *always* refer back to the note immediately preceding them. See section 4.5 for a discussion of simpler ways to handle multiple references.

What if the passage that I want to quote is very long? If you feel you must quote a lengthy passage, then you should go back and discuss the elements you think are crucial for your argument. You should not assume that the reader will draw the same conclusions from the passage that you do. You need to talk the reader through the passage to draw his or her attention to the key elements of the material. Which parts of the quotation are the most useful evidence for your case? Explain this in your own words. Remember that you can also edit a lengthy passage as long as you make it clear to the reader what you have done, and as long as you don't change the meaning of the passage. Replace any words you omit with ellipses enclosed within square brackets: [...].

If I find a quotation in a book, should I cite the original source of the quotation or the book I found it in? The original source of the quotation should be included in your citation. You must also provide a proper citation to the source where *you* found the quotation. The original source therefore appears as "quoted in" in the secondary source. Here is how such a citation would appear as a footnote. Note that this source is a multi-authored volume, so there are three distinct sources here: the quotation from Umberto Eco appears in Paul DePasquale's essay, which appears in the book edited by Jennifer Brown and Elizabeth Vibert.

Sample Footnote

⁵ Umberto Eco, *Serendipities: Language and Lunacy,* trans. William Weaver (New York: Columbia University Press, 1998), 54–55. Quoted in Paul DePasquale, "'Worth the Noting': European Ambivalence and Aboriginal Agency in Meta Incognita, 1576–1578," in *Reading Beyond Words: Contexts for Native History,* 2nd ed., ed. Jennifer S. H. Brown and Elizabeth Vibert (Peterborough: Broadview Press, 2003), 9.

Here is another example of a primary source, an interview with Mao Zedong, which has been quoted by Mao himself in a later collection of his essays. The 1936 interview is mentioned together with the title of the essay (in quotation marks), and the title of the book in which it was published in 1967 (in italics).

CITATION

Sample Footnote

[6] Mao Zedong, interview with Edgar Snow, 16 July 1936, quoted in "On Protracted War," *Selected Works of Mao Zedong*, Vol. II (Peking: Foreign Languages Press, 1967), 120.

If I use endnotes rather than footnotes, do I still need a bibliography? Yes. All research essays require both a list of references and another, separate, alphabetized list of all the sources you have cited. The citations refer to the sources one at a time and provide specific page numbers for the reader, and some sources may be cited many times. On the other hand, your bibliography provides a concise list of all the sources.

4.2 PLAGIARISM

Throughout this guide, we emphasize the way that all academic work builds on the work of others. Historical writing inevitably makes use of primary and secondary sources and in this sense is never entirely "original." Good historical writing, however, always clearly acknowledges the sources on which it is based. If you fail to acknowledge those sources, you are effectively presenting someone else's work as though it were your own. Doing so constitutes *plagiarism*—the theft of someone else's words or ideas. Plagiarism is one of the most serious academic offences.

Plagiarism can take many forms. Copying an entire essay by downloading it from a website or by reproducing it from a book or from any work by someone else is the most obvious. Copying paragraphs and sentences from other sources and pasting them together with a handful of linking words or sentences without proper attribution also constitutes plagiarism. Copying material from websites and failing to cite your source properly is also plagiarism. (This is also very poor research.) Taking a paper written for one class and handing it in to another professor as though it were new work is also a form of academic dishonesty, and many institutions define it as plagiarism and treat it with equal severity.

To avoid plagiarism, distinctive phrases and concepts that have not yet entered into general use should always be presented in quotation marks and properly documented. When you take the substance of an argument or an account of events from another source—even when you are not quoting directly and have put it into your own words—you need to provide a clear acknowledgment of that source. (See Chapter 3,

CITATION

section 3.7B, on quoting and paraphrasing, for more information on appropriate ways to paraphrase.)

As we noted earlier in this chapter, things that are commonly known do not require documentation. Deciding what is or is not "common knowledge" is a matter of judgment and varies with context. Because textbooks represent the current state of their field, much of the material you find there can be understood to be common knowledge. If all of the secondary sources you consult present certain ideas or information as uncontroversial and without documenting their sources for them, then you can similarly assume that these ideas and information are common knowledge. If you are in doubt, consult your instructor for guidance. In general, if you have any doubt, it is better to provide a citation.

Material presented in lectures presents a special case. Sometimes that material (like material in the textbook) is common knowledge. In other cases, the lecture may draw on specific authors or works that require citation. If you want to cite material presented in a lecture, you should ask your instructor where you can find a source for that information and then cite the source directly. If she or he tells you that the information can be found in any textbook, then it is common knowledge and does not require citation.

Most institutions have formal policies on plagiarism, and you should be aware of the policies in place at your college or university. You should also be aware that many institutions now use sophisticated computer software to detect plagiarism. The penalties for plagiarism vary with the seriousness of the offence. In some cases, a grade of zero may be assigned for the paper in question; more serious cases may merit the student's suspension or expulsion and a permanent note on his or her record.

4.3 CITATION STYLES

Most historians use *Chicago style for the humanities*, developed by the University of Chicago and described in *The Chicago Manual of Style*, currently in its Fifteenth Edition. Visit **www.chicagomanualofstyle.org** for more information. Other disciplines use other style guides. For example, most work in languages and literature uses *MLA style*, developed by the Modern Language Association, a nonprofit organization that promotes the teaching and study of literature and language. See **www.mla.org/style** if you would like more information.

Chicago style for the humanities allows you to place bibliographic citations at the bottom of the page as *footnotes* or at the end of a paper as *endnotes*. It also provides a slightly different format for your *bibliography*,

CITATION

which must be included at the very end of your paper for the reader's information. In some cases, you may use a *works cited* page instead of a bibliography. A bibliography is an alphabetized summary of all of the sources you have consulted during the investigation of your topic; a works cited list includes only those works actually cited in your paper.

Whether you choose to use the Chicago or some other recognized style, what is most important is that you use the chosen style *consistently* throughout your paper. Keeping your citation format consistent is a key feature of a well-presented and well-documented argument, and it helps the reader review your source material easily. Because the Chicago style is the one most commonly used by historians, we have provided a series of basic examples in Chicago style in section 4.4, below.

Students sometimes ask whether they can use in-text citations, the way they do in science and social science papers. In-text citations, such as those used in the APA style (developed by the American Psychological Association) and CSE style (developed by the Council of Science Editors) are generally not appropriate in history papers or journals. One of the main reasons is that the kinds of sources historians use—for example, a diary entry or a newspaper article from the 1890s—require complicated citations that are difficult to incorporate into the text. (Where in-text citations are used, they typically appear in parentheses at the end of a sentence.) Some instructors, however, permit the use of in-text citations, especially if the paper involves interdisciplinary work. Consult your instructor or teaching assistant.

4.4 BASIC CITATION EXAMPLES FOR FOOTNOTES/ENDNOTES AND BIBLIOGRAPHIES IN CHICAGO STYLE

Remember that your paper must provide bibliographic citations for quotations and paraphrased material in the form of footnotes or endnotes, as well as a comprehensive bibliography at the end of the paper. Do *not* list items in the bibliography in the order in which they were cited. The entries in the bibliography should be alphabetized according to the author's last name. Below, we offer examples of citations for some common types of sources in Chicago style, showing the correct format for both footnotes/endnotes and bibliographic entries. These entries reflect the format required for the *first time* such sources are cited. Subsequent citations may be simplified (see section 4.5). Note that the first line of a footnote/endnote entry is indented, while in a bibliographic entry, the second and subsequent lines are indented instead; the latter type of indentation is called a "hanging indent."

CITATION

A) BOOKS BY A SINGLE AUTHOR, CO-AUTHORS, OR A CORPORATION

- Footnote or Endnote:

    [6] Gene Kranz, *Failure Is Not an Option: Mission Control from Mercury to Apollo 13 and Beyond* (New York: Simon & Schuster, 2000), 169–70.

- Bibliography:

    Kranz, Gene. *Failure Is Not an Option: Mission Control from Mercury to Apollo 13 and Beyond.* New York: Simon & Schuster, 2000.

BOOKS WITH AN EDITOR OR TRANSLATOR

In edited or translated works, the author's name comes first and the editor's or translator's name comes after the title.

- Footnote or Endnote:

    [7] Mary Wollstonecraft, *The Vindications: The Rights of Men and the Rights of Woman*, ed. D. L. Macdonald and Kathleen Scherf (Peterborough, ON: Broadview Press, 1997).

- Bibliography:

    Wollstonecraft, Mary. *The Vindications: The Rights of Men and the Rights of Woman.* Edited by D. L. Macdonald and Kathleen Scherf. Peterborough, ON: Broadview Press, 1997.

B) JOURNAL ARTICLES

- Footnote or Endnote:

    [8] Susan Ferguson, "The Radical Ideas of Mary Wollstonecraft," *Canadian Journal of Political Science* 32, no. 3 (September 1999): 50.

- Bibliography:

    Ferguson, Susan. "The Radical Ideas of Mary Wollstonecraft." *Canadian Journal of Political Science* 32, no. 3 (September 1999): 427–51.

C) NEWSPAPER AND MAGAZINE ARTICLES

- Footnote or Endnote:

    [9] "Ruling on 1760 Treaty May Aid Tribal Claims," *The Gazette* (Montreal, QC), September 11, 1987, final edition.

CITATION

NEL

- Bibliography:

  Newspaper articles are not normally cited individually in the bibliography if they have been properly cited in the text itself. If you have drawn a number of articles from one newspaper, you list the newspaper in your bibliography as follows:

  The Gazette (Montreal, QC)

D) ARTICLES OR CHAPTERS IN A MULTI-AUTHOR WORK

- Footnote or Endnote:

  [10] Daniel Clayton, "Captain Cook and the Spaces of Contact at Nootka Sound," in *Reading Beyond Words: Contexts for Native History*, 2nd ed., ed. Jennifer S. H. Brown and Elizabeth Vibert (Peterborough: Broadview Press, 2003), 133–62.

- Bibliography:

  Clayton, Daniel. "Captain Cook and the Spaces of Contact at Nootka Sound." In *Reading Beyond Words: Contexts for Native History*, 2nd ed., edited by Jennifer S. H. Brown and Elizabeth Vibert, 133–62. Peterborough: Broadview Press, 2003.

E) ONLINE SOURCES AND E-JOURNALS

- Footnote or Endnote:

  [11] David R. Williams, "The Apollo Program (1963–1972)," National Aeronautics and Space Administration, http://nssdc.gsfc.nasa.gov/planetary/lunar/apollo.html (accessed 30 October 2008).

- Bibliography:

  Williams, David R. "The Apollo Program (1963–1972)." National Aeronautics and Space Administration. http://nssdc.gsfc.nasa.gov/planetary/lunar/apollo.html (accessed 30 October 2008).

Note: There is a special format for citing articles that you find using online databases like EBSCO, JSTOR, LexisNexis, InfoTrac, etc. In this case, provide the citation or bibliographic entry as well as the permanent URL, followed by the date you accessed the material.

- Footnote or Endnote:

  [12] Diana Coole, "Re-reading Political Theory from a Woman's Perspective," *Political Studies* 34, 1 (March 1986): 130. http://search.ebscohost.com/login.aspx?direct=true&db=a9h&AN=21376580&site=ehost-live (accessed 30 October 2008).

CITATION

- Bibliography:

Coole, Diana. "Re-reading Political Theory from a Woman's
  Perspective." *Political Studies* 34, 1 (March 1986): 129–48.
  http://search.ebscohost.com/login.aspx?direct=true&db=a9h&AN=
  21376580&site=ehost-live (accessed 30 October 2008).

F) ONLINE VIDEO CLIPS

If you are citing a video clip that you have seen online, such as on a news
media site, then use the following format when providing a reference to
that source. Provide the name of the author, artist, director, composer, or
producer, if available; the title of the work or the name of the file in
quotation marks; any relevant publication information; the publication
date or the date the file was modified (if known); the full Web address;
and the date you viewed the clip.

- Footnote or Endnote:

[14] Information Telegraph Agency of Russia (ITAR-TASS), "R-7 ICBM
Launching Sputnik-1 from Baikonur," (October 1957). YouTube.
http://www.youtube.com/watch?v=qcex_MuBT7Y (accessed 30 October 2008).

If you do use a video clip from an old newsreel or a speech on YouTube
or similar sites you must ensure that it is authentic and provide as much
information about it as you can.

It is your responsibility to ensure that any online sources you have
used are accurately cited. For a complete listing of online source citation
formats, consult *The Chicago Manual of Style*. As a general rule, you
should strive to make your citations for Internet sources as detailed and
comprehensive as possible. The site address, or URL, is a critical detail
and should not be omitted. In cases where the information may be
updated or is especially time-sensitive, the date of consultation must also
be included.

G) GOVERNMENT PUBLICATIONS

- Footnote or Endnote:

[15] William David Compton, *Where No Man Has Gone Before: A History of
Apollo Lunar Exploration Missions,* National Aeronautics and Space Administration,
NASA SP; 4214 (Washington: United States Government Printing Office, 1989),
146–48.

- Bibliography:

Compton, William David. *Where No Man Has Gone Before: A History
  of Apollo Lunar Exploration Missions.* National Aeronautics and
  Space Administration, NASA SP; 4214. Washington: United
  States Government Printing Office, 1989.

CITATION

H) VIDEO RECORDINGS, CDS, AND DVDS

- Footnote or Endnote:

    [16] Discovery Channel, *One Giant Leap: The Heroic Story of Mankind's First Landing on the Moon,* VHS (Bethesda, MD: Alliance Video, 1994).

- Bibliography:

    Discovery Channel. *One Giant Leap: The Heroic Story of Mankind's First Landing on the Moon.* VHS. Bethesda, MD: Alliance Video, 1994.

I) OTHER SOURCES

Visual materials, if found in any of the above sources, can generally be cited as above, with the inclusion of appropriate page numbers or URLs. Citations for artifacts and oral histories are complex, so if you wish to cite these sources, consult *The Chicago Manual of Style.* You should also speak with your instructor.

4.5 SUBSEQUENT CITATIONS FOR FOOTNOTES AND ENDNOTES: THE SHORTCUTS

After a source has been cited in full, and you wish to cite it again in another footnote or endnote, you don't need to provide another full bibliographic entry. You should simplify the entry by including only the last name(s) of the author(s) and the page number. Where two or more sources by the same author are being cited, include a shortened version of the title also, in order to distinguish between the two.

- Footnote or Endnote:

    [13] Kranz, 221.

or

    [13] Kranz, *Failure Is Not an Option,* 221.

4.6 CITATION CHECKLIST

Here is a checklist to help you format your citations and avoid doing unnecessary work.

- Use a recognized citation style and use it consistently (we recommend Chicago style for the humanities).

CITATION

- Do not use APA style citations, such as: (Smith, 2003) unless your instructor explicitly allows them. In-text citations are not usually appropriate in history papers. Insert footnotes or endnotes using MS Word's insert-reference feature.

- Do not use Roman numerals (i, ii, iii) for references—use Arabic numerals (1, 2, 3).

- Always *italicize* book and periodical titles in your references and bibliography:
  - *A Modern History of Japan*
  - *The Journal of U.S. History*
  - *The Gazette*
  - *The People's Daily*

- If there are two quotations from the same source, you still need only one reference number.

- Quotations of one or two sentences should be run into your text.

- Quotations *more than two sentences* long must appear as offset, or "block" quotations, which are entirely indented on *the left side*, and need no quotation marks.

Conclusion

Writing well is hard work. It requires careful thought at every stage, as well as meticulous planning and careful editing. You need to think about every sentence and try to determine whether it could do its job more effectively or more efficiently. The reward for that effort is not only better grades in history courses, but the ability to read more critically and to think and write more clearly and effectively—skills that will benefit you in many areas of life. As you read the articles and books your instructors assign in history courses, pay attention not only to what the authors say, but also to *how* they say it. Look for examples of good thesis statements, clear arguments, and effective conclusions in the historical work that you read. The more reading you do the better your own writing will become, and the more you think about and work on your writing, the more effective it will be.

As we suggested in the introduction to this guide, learning to write good history essays means learning to write like a historian. Once you have learned how to do that—once you have mastered the rules and principles that govern good historical writing—then you will have taken the first step from being a history student to being a historian yourself. At that point, you may decide that you want to begin to break some of these rules and challenge the ways that historians think and write. This is how disciplines develop and change. Each generation produces new histories, not because the past has changed, but because it approaches that past from a new perspective, with new questions and new techniques. We hope that this guide may encourage some of you to join us in that project.

For Further Reading

This work is designed to be a practical guide to aid you with the researching, formulating, and writing of research essays in history. It focuses principally on the mechanics of conducting an investigation, structuring an argument, and building an effective case that will persuade the reader. For further information on grammatical structures, writing style, and the use of punctuation, you should refer to the following sources, which discuss these subjects in further detail.

Buckley, Joanne. *Checkmate: A Writing Reference for Canadians.* Scarborough, ON: Nelson, 2007.

The Chicago Manual of Style. 15th ed. Chicago: University of Chicago Press, 2003.

Finnbogason, Jack, and Al Valleau. *A Canadian Writer's Guide.* 4th ed. Toronto, ON: Nelson, 2010.

Gibaldi, Joseph. *The MLA Handbook for Writers of Research Papers.* 6th ed. New York: Modern Language Association of America, 2006.

Heckman, Grant. *The Nelson Guide to Essay Writing.* Scarborough, ON: Nelson, 2002.

Rosenwasser, David, Jill Stephen, and Douglas Babbington. *Writing Analytically.* Scarborough, ON: Nelson, 2005.

For a study of academic writing more broadly, see Janet Giltrow, *Academic Writing*, 3rd ed. (Peterborough, ON: Broadview Press, 2002).

Index

little-known facts, 82, 83
long, essay-style answers, 33–34
long quotations, 84, 92

M
magazine articles, 3, 88–89
making a case, 54, 55
maps, 22
marginalized groups, 16
material culture, 16–17
medieval history online resources, 10–11
meta-search engine, 8
mixed metaphors, 71
MLA style, 86
Modern Language Association, 86
monographs. *See* historical monographs
multi-authored volume, 84, 89
museum exhibits, 5

N
names, 69, 75
national names, 69
"Nature, Reason and Equality in Mary Wollstonecraft's *A Vindication of the Rights of Woman*" (sample essay 2), 38, 40–41, 42, 52–53, 55–56, 57–58, 72–73
New York Times, 10
news organizations, 15
newspaper articles, 3, 4–5, 88–89
note-taking, careless, 43
the novel, 5
numbers, 74–75

O
obscure facts, 82
obvious claims, 49
official titles, 68–69
online sources
    African history, 10
    ancient and medieval history, 10–11
    Canadian history, 11
    citation, 9–10, 89–90
    databases, 89–90
    described, 7–10
    European history, 11–12
    film clips, 15

Latin American history, 12
    U.S. history, 12
    validity of, 9
    video clips, 90
    visual sources, 13
oral histories, 17–18, 91
organization of thoughts, 54–55
"The Origins of Communist China: Mao Zedong and the War of Resistance against Japan, 1937-45" (sample essay 4), 38, 53–54, 58–59, 61, 62–63, 65–66, 71–72
outline, 59
Oxford English Dictionary, 45

P
paragraphs, 56
paraphrasing, 65–66
parliamentary proceedings, 3
passive voice, 70
past tense, 68
periodicals, 3, 4–5, 88–89, 92
personal journals, 3
photographs, 12
physical objects, 16
plagiarism, 10, 43, 85–86
planning your paper, 54–56
point-form structure, 56
police records, 3
political cartoons, 12
portraits, 12
précis, 27
presentation of evidence, 59–67
primary source analysis, 27–28, 38
primary sources
    described, 2, 3–4
    as evidence, 62
    quotations from, found in secondary sources, 62, 64, 84
    reading primary sources, 44–49
Project Muse®, 8
proofreading, 77–79, 78–79
proposals, research, 34–35
punctuation, 82

Q
Questia, 8
questions, development of, 41–42
quotation of sources

appropriate use of quotation, 63
block quotation, 65, 92
direct quotation, 62–64, 82, 83
inappropriate use of quotation, 63
long quotations, 84, 92
primary *vs.* secondary sources, 62
quote within quote, 64
secondary sources, 64, 65, 66
short quotations, 92
of source in secondary source, 84

R

rare book collections, 3
read work aloud, 78
reading responses, 25–26
"recognizes," 48, 67
references, 82
relevance of evidence, 63
religious names, 69
report, 51
rereading your paper, 79
research essay
    argument, development of, 49–54
    body of paper, 59–67
    building your case, 60–61
    conclusions, 71–73
    define your terms, 66–67
    described, 35–36
    editing, 75–76
    elements of, 35–36
    example of, 38
    format of, 74–76
    grading, 79–80
    introduction, 57–59
    paraphrasing, 65–66
    pitfalls to avoid, 69–71
    planning your paper, 54–56
    presentation of evidence, 59–67
    proofreading, 77–79
    questions, development of, 41–42
    quoting sources, 62–65
    reading your sources, 44–49
    research, 41–42
    sample essays. *See* sample research
      essays
    thesis statement, 49–54
    tips, 68–69
    title of paper, 76–77
    title page, 77

topic, selection of, 39–41
word choices, 67
writing for your audience, 67–71
research for paper, 41–42
research proposals, 34–35

S

sample research essays
    introduction, 38–39
    "Nature, Reason and Equality in
      Mary Wollstonecraft's *A*
      Vindication of the Rights of
      Woman" (essay 2), 38, 40–41,
      42, 52–53, 55–56, 57–58,
      72–73
    "The Origins of Communist
      China: Mao Zedong and the
      War of Resistance against
      Japan, 1937-45" (essay 4), 38,
      53–54, 58–59, 61, 62–63,
      65–66, 71–72
    "Stories of Contact: Debates in
      First Nations' History" (essay
      3), 38, 47–48, 64–65, 72–73
    "Technology Innovation and the
      Apollo Program" (essay 1), 38,
      51–52, 60–61, 76–77
sample research worksheet, 45–46
Second World War, 18
secondary source analysis, 31
secondary sources
    described, 2, 5–7, 19
    as evidence, 62
    paraphrasing, 65
    primary sources quoted in, 62, 64,
      84
    quotations from, 64, 65, 66
    reading secondary sources, 47–49
self-references, 70
sensationalist topics, 40
several facts or ideas, 83
short exam answers, 31–33
"sic," 65
simple words, 68
slang phrases, 70–71
sources
    artifacts, 16–17, 22
    and bias, 44–45
    critical reading, importance of, 2